Black&White Graphics. (Black&Why#1) A book edited by Andrea Lugli.

First published in 2003 by **CRUCIX-SHOP**.
Via Provinciale per Modena 132/A, 41016 Novi di Modena (MO), Italy - Telephone +39 059 670767 - crucify@crucix-shop.com - www.crucix-shop.com

Distributed Worldwide (except Italy) by:

GINGKO PRESS INC.
5768 Paradise Drive, Suite J
Corte Madera, CA 94925, USA
Telephone (415) 924-9615
Telefax (415) 924-9608
Email: books@gingkopress.com
www.gingkopress.com

Copyright © 2003 Crucix-Shop
Book Design: Andrea Lugli Design.

All right reserved. No part of this publication may be reproduced, stored in retrieval systems or transmitted in any form or by any means, electronic or mechanical, including photocopying, recording or any information storage and retrieval systems, without permission in writing from the publisher and the copyright owners.
Gingko Press 1-58423-149-1
Crucix-Shop 88-901082-0-7
Printed in Italy by EBS, Verona.

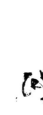

B&W Graphics

andrea lugli presents

CONTENTS

001	
002-003	Colophon
004-005	CONTENTS
006-007	AUTHORS
008-009	FOREWORD – BY FONS Matthias HICKMANN
010-011	
012-013	
014-019	EMIGRE – RUDY VANDERLANS
020-025	ED FELLA
026-031	DIRK RUDOLPH
032-037	GAIL SWANLUND
038-043	WHY NOT ASSOCIATES
044-049	ANDREA LUGLI
050-055	STEPHEN FARRELL
056-061	JENNIFER STERLING
062-069	STEFAN SAGMEISTER
070-073	MAROK
074-079	SHEPARD FAIREY
080-085	ROBERTO BAGATTI
086-091	URS ALTHAUS
092-097	MARCUS BURLILE
098-103	PLAZM
104-115	DEAN KARR

116-121	GEOFF KAPLAN
122-127	HAND GUN
128-133	FRANK HEINE (U.O.R.G.)
134-139	FONS M. HICKMANN
140-145	CAROLINE ABELE
146-151	RAFFAELE PRIMITIVO
152-157	PLANET PIXEL
158-163	BENJAMIN GÜDEL
164-169	ERIC FENG
170-171	GESINE GROTRIAN-STEINWEG
172-177	APT 13
178-181	MARTIN WOODTLI
182-187	ENRICO BRAVI
188-197	TOMATO
198-203	KIM HIORTHØY
204-213	DARREN SCOTT
214-215	
216-217	Backword – BY Andrea Lugli
218-221	BIOGRAPHIES
222-223	CONTACTS
224	TYPE IN BLACK&WHITE GRAPHICS

authors

Caroline Abile 140-145
Urs Althaus 86-91
Apt.13 172-177
Roberto Bagatti 80-85
Enrico Bravi 102-107
Marcus Burlile 92-97
Emigre (Rudy VanderLans) 14-19
Shepard Fairey 74-79
Stephen Farrell 50-55
Edward Fella 20-25
Eric Feng 164-169

- Cesil Grotrian-Stilweg 170-171
- Benjamin Güdel 158-163
- Haldgun 122-127
- Frank Heine 128-133
- Fons M. Hickmann 134-139
- Kim Hiorthøy 198-203
- Geoff Kaplan 116-121
- Dean Karr 104-115
- Andrea Lugli 44-49 (62-69, 104-115, 188-197, 204-213)
- Narok 70-73
- Planet Pixel 152-157
- Plazm 98-103
- Raffaele Primitivo 146-151
- Dirk Rudolph 26-31
- Stefan Sagmeister 62-69
- Darren Scott 204-213
- Jennifer Sterling 56-61
- Gail Swanlund 32-37
- Tomato 188-197
- Why not associates 38-43
- Martin Woodtli 178-181

Foreword by Fons M. Hi<!--ckmann-->

EVERYTHING WILL BE IN BLACK AND WHITE.

BLACK AND **WHITE** ARE NOT COLOURS, BUT A PHILOSOPHY. MOREOVER, AS BOTH **AVOID A CLEAR CHROMATIC DEFINITION**, THEY

LET **US** REMAIN INITIALLY IN THE **FIELD** OF **COLOUR THEORY** AND DEAL WITH THE MEDIA OF RELEVANCE TO THE WORK OF D FOR THE PRODUCTION OF PRINTED MATTER. THE ADDITION OF JUST A FEW COLOUR GLAZES, GENERALLY **FOUR** IN TOTAL, ALLO **ONE** ON TOP OF one another, GIVES YOU A **DEEP BLACK**. HOWEVER, **BEFORE** THE DESIGNER PRINTS SOMETHING, IN GENERAL BECAUSE **THE MONITOR WORKS WITH LIGHT**. ONLY THREE COLOURS ARE USED ON A COMPUTER MONITOR, AND **WHERE THESE OVE**

Black AND white REPRESENT CONCENTRATIONS, CONCENTRATIONS TRANSPORTED BY COLOUR. BLACK AND WHITE **CONDENSE** EVER

IF ONE ACCEPTS THIS PRINCIPLE, IT **BECOMES EVIDENT** THAT AS FAR AS THE PHENOMENON OF BLACK AND WHITE **IS CO** MORE **MULTIFACETED** THAN BLACK AND WHITE, **THE REST** IS **MERELY** COLOURFUL. AND, IRRESPECTIVE OF THE **VIRTUOS** CAN BE QUANTIFIED, BLACK AND WHITE ARE **INFINITE**.

THE IMMEASURABLE **NATURE** OF BLACK AND WHITE AND THE MANNER IN WHICH THEY **ESCAPE CLASSIFICATION** GUARANTEES **FORCES**. THEY SPREAD THE **TERROR** felt by an AUTHOR FACING THE **DEATHLY WHITE** OF AN **EMPTY PAGE**, THE AN AND THE DREAD AMONG POLITICIANS OF A MENTAL BLACK-OUT.

HOPES ARE PINNED ON **WHITE BRIDAL GOWNS** AND **BLACK UNDERWEAR**. WE CALL OIL, "BLACK GOLD" AND IT IS SOLD B AND **PRAY** FOR THE IMMACULATE CONCEPTION. DOVES OF PEACE AND ANGELS HOVER AROUND **OUR** HEADS, WHILE WE SEE

BLACK AND WHITE ARE **DIALECTIC** principles. ON THE **ONE** HAND, THIS MEANS THAT WE ATTAIN COMPACTION THROUGH CHOOSE. BECAUSE THE PRINCIPLES OF **BLACK** AND **WHITE** ENCOMPASS EVERYTHING, THEY ARE **IDEAL** AS INTERPRETATION SU A **SPHERE** FOR THE IMAGINATION, A FANTASY WORLD, A landscape OF **LONGING** AND **DREAMS**.

FOR THIS REASON, **I WOULD PLEAD** THAT IN THE FUTURE ALL televisions, displays, **ILLUMINATED** SIGNS AND COMPUTER

FONS M. HICKMANN, BERLIN/VIENNA

AN BE REGARDED IN PROGRAMMATIC TERMS.

GNERS. FIRSTLY, THERE IS THE ADDITIVE **COLOUR SYSTEM** TO BE CONSIDERED, WHICH FOR EXAMPLE, IS employed
E ATTAINMENT **OF INNUMERABLE NUANCES** BY MEANS OF OVERPRINTING. THE PRINTING OF **ALL FOUR** COLOUR
SHE WORKS WITH A COMPUTER, in which everything functions IN PRECISELY THE **REVERSE** FASHION. THIS IS
, THE RESULT IS A BRILLIANT WHITE.

ECE OF INFORMATION. BLACK AND WHITE CONSTITUTE **AN EXTRACT**, COMPOSED **OF THE SUM** OF ALL INFORMATION.

ERNED, ONE SHOULD **not** REFER TO THE monochromatic BUT TO THE **FULL CHROMATIC**. THERE IS NOTHING
IAT THEY SOMETIMES DISPLAY, COLOURS CONSTITUTE LIMITED TONALITY AND BREADTH OF INFORMATION. COLOUR

ERTAIN **IRRITATION**. THEY CREATE FANTASIES CONCERNING the omnipotence OF **UNCONTROLLABLE, SUBVERSIVE**
TY OF THE FILM DIRECTOR CONFRONTING A BLACK SCREEN, THE **FEAR** OF SOLDIERS WHEN HOISTING A **WHITE FLAG**

EN IN **WHITE TURBANS** TO **DEALERS** WITH **WHITER THAN WHITE REPUTATIONS**. WE ARE SUCKED INTO BLACK HOLES
THE PATH OF ENLIGHTENMENT IN THE **DARKNESS** OF NIGHT.

COMPRESSION OF INFORMATION, BUT ON THE **OTHER**, THAT WE CAN ALSO extrapolate any information THAT WE
ACES ONTO WHICH **ANYTHING CAN BE WRITTEN** AND FROM WHICH **EVERYTHING CAN BE READ**. BLACK AND WHITE REPRESENT

MONITORS SHOULD BE **WHITE** AND THAT ALL NEWSPAPERS, POSTERS AND BOOKS SHOULD BE **BLACK**.

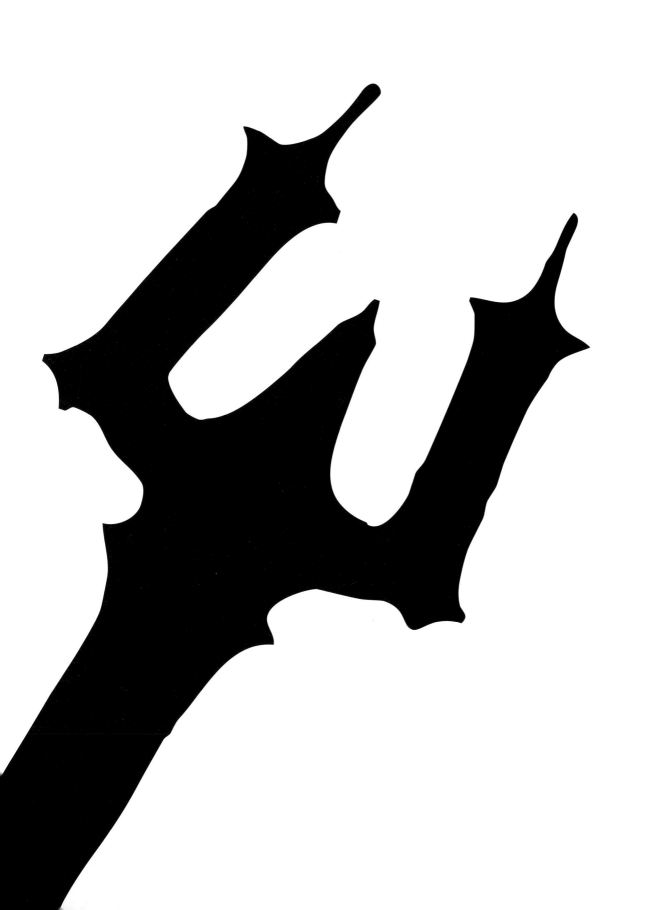

AN INTERVIEW WITH RUDY VANDERLANS IN BLACK & WHITE

SET IN FAIRPLEX (Beta Version), A NEW TYPEFACE DESIGNED BY ZUZANA LICKO

FAIRPLEX WIDE BLACK
& WIDE BLACK ITALIC

Interview by *Dave Mandl*

FAIRPLEX WIDE BLACK
& WIDE BLACK ITALIC

FAIRPLEX WIDE BOLD
& WIDE BOLD ITALIC

Rudy VanderLans is editor of the graphic design magazine *Emigre*, and co-founder of the digital type foundry of the same name. He recently published *Joshue Tree*, the third in a series of books presenting photographs taken of the Southern California (SoCal) landscape. The trilogy was inspired by the music of the area's legendary pop geniuses, including Van Dyke Parks (who collaborated with Brian Wilson on his masterpiece, *Smile*), Captain Beefheart, and flamboyant country-rock founding father Gram Parsons. Included with all the books are CDs of music by Parks and former members of Beefheart's Magic Band, new interpretations of Parks's songs, and field recordings made in the SoCal area.

FAIRPLEX NARROW BOLD
NARROW BOOK
& NARROW BOOK ITALIC

Dave: Emigre was at the forefront of the digital-design boom of the '90s. And much of the '90s art/design culture seemed to want to get as far away as possible from the physical body and the organic world. But your recent work in the California trilogy couldn't be more different from that aesthetic, with very literal analog photographs of the natural landscape, and simple, understated production. Is this a new direction or a change of heart for you, a reaction to an overdose of digitality and technology, perhaps?

Rudy: Yes, to an extend it is a reaction to an overdose of technology. Although, make no mistake about this, these books are designed on a computer, the photographs were scanned by computers, and printed by presses that are fully computerized. But I'm trying hard to make them look otherwise. So these books are also mired in the traditions of typographic convention and bookmaking, with much attention paid to the physical qualities of the book. Many parts are still assembled by hand, such as the endsheets, head and tail bands, case binding, embossing, etc. Plus the CD and small wrappers are added by hand. I'm not interested any more in letting the technology dictate what to do, because when you do you run the risk that everything starts looking the same.

Furthermore, these books deal with a desire I have to connect with what is indigenous to California. I want these books to look like they were made in California. Lately, within my own profession of graphic design, I have sensed a serious decrease of work that feels indigenous, work that holds qualities that are particular to a certain region or country where the work is made. I get work send to me from New York, Tokyo, Amsterdam or Singapore, and often it is impossible to detect where it comes from.

A good example of an artist who wears his immediate environment on his sleeve is Ed Ruscha. You look at much of his work and it just exudes Los Angeles.

When you own one of his pieces, it's like owning a piece of Los Angeles. That's what I really like about Ed Ruscha, and it's what I like to bring into my own work. So I started touring around California with my camera and see what is still unique about this place, and how I can incorporate bits and pieces of that into my work.

Dave: After more than a century of industrialization, the desert is still a constant presence in California; even in the densest urban landscape, it seems you can't drive a mile without seeing it poking through somewhere. In most other American urban centers, however (New York, say), the natural landscape has been long buried. Do you think the omnipresence of the desert in California allows people to retain some psychic connection to the "real" California, or to the natural world, even in a megalopolis like L.A.?

Rudy: That's a beautiful thought. And if you're open to that idea, there's much to enjoy in that regard. You can walk into the Santa Monica Mountains, Griffith's Park, let's say, and if it's a hazy day and you squint your eyes, and you look towards downtown, you may get a sense of what L.A. used to look like around the turn of the century. But for the most part people like to pave things over. Most vegetation you see in Los Angeles is not indigenous. For many people in L.A. the desert is this long stretch of no man's land you drive through real fast on your way to Las Vegas. And developers seem to consider the desert, just like they did the valleys before, as the last cheap frontier to expand the outer reaches of L.A. into. I can't imagine they have any interest in the natural world that surrounds them. I'm sure they're very aware of it, but only in terms of its tremendous and often devastating powers. It doesn't always easily comply with man's need to pave it over. Floods, earthquakes, mudslides, terrible heat and cold, and desert storms can make living in, or close to, a desert environment a very unpleasant experience. Rattlesnakes and coyotes still find their way down the canyons into people's backyards. To many, that's simply a nuisance, not anything to be in awe of or to connect to. It's something to conquer, like cementing the banks of the Los Angeles river from its source in The San Fernando Valley, all the way to where it spills out into San Pedro Bay.

Dave: You talk about being drawn to sites with historical or "mystical" significance for you – like the former sites of Zappa's studio and Beefheart's workspace – even though they're now populated by nondescript suburban buildings. Are there some kinds of "traces" or "ghosts" remaining in these places? Can they be detected? Can photos capture them?

Rudy: This, to me, is the most exciting part of these photo trips. To see if anything is left behind that may hint at the greatness that these spots were witness to. Or perhaps to see what it is that attracted these artists to be in these particular places. That's exactly the reason I go to these places in the first place. The expectations are huge, always. These trips are like little pilgrimages. Of course, it's usually a disappointment. Most of the time there's nothing there of any significance. On the contrary. But what's always there are the stories, the histories that surround them that make these places interesting. And that is what these books are about. They're trying to extend the stories, or to keep the stories alive. Or, at the very least, to provide the stories with a visual backdrop.

Dave: Similarly, do you think there are traces of the old SoCal landscape, which, as you say, is being slowly replaced by faceless suburban homes, that are somehow preserved in *Song Cycle*, the music of Gram Parsons, etc.? Do you see this music as a kind of time capsule, so that combining a listen to *Sweetheart of the Rodeo* with a road trip through the present-day SoCal landscape helps bring the SoCal of thirty years ago back to life?

Rudy: I'm not interested in bringing these times back to life. That would be impossible anyway. But I am

FAIRPLEX NARROW BOLD
NARROW BOOK
& NARROW BOOK ITALIC

PAGE FROM AN IMAGINARY BOOK

Fig. 16   *Fig. 17*   *Fig. 18*

FROM LEFT TO RIGHT:
Song Cycle, Van Dyke Parks. Album design by Ed Trasher. Photography by Guy Webster.
Trout Mask Replica, Captain Beefheart and His Magic Band. Album design by Cal Schenkel with Ed Caraeff.
Sweetheart of the Rodeo, The Byrds (with Gram Parsons). Album design by Geller and Butler Advertising. Illustration by Jo Mora.

interested in showing what was really good about them. And show how things have changed. But, at the same time, I do think that, like all great art, an album like *Song Cycle* represents and preserves a particular time and place. Particularly the original vinyl version. It does this by the way it sounds technically, by the way it was recorded, by its physical qualities as a piece of vinyl, by its subject matter, by the artists and engineers who produced the album, by the cover design and the designer and photographer who produced it. All this ties the album to a particular time and place. All these qualities are preserved in *Song Cycle*. It's an artifact. And as such it has come to represent the California of 1968. But what makes an album like *Song Cycle* truly great is that the music transcends all this. *Song Cycle* is timeless. This sounds like a paradox, but it isn't. The music itself, I feel, is timeless, because it was never tied to any particular trend.

Of course the great risk in doing these three books was to have them all be dismissed as a sad, sappy, nostalgic road trip by some midlifer. And I can't deny I don't derive some sentimental pleasures from doing this. But I also wanted to bring attention to these musicians and in particular these three albums. And to pay homage to them. To me, the three albums that inspired these books, *Song Cycle*, *Sweetheart of the Rodeo*, and *Trout Mask Replica*, are the three most important pop music albums ever made. And they have quite a bit in common. They were all released around 1968, and all three stand in stark contrast to the bulk of pop albums put out at the time. And not only are they artistically unique, they were obviously great risks for both the artists and record companies to release at that time. And what I admire most about these three albums is that they offered something original while remaining firmly grounded in the traditions of indigenous American music. *Song Cycle*, one could argue, was inspired by the music of American composers like Copland and Gershwin. *Trout Mask Replica* is mired in the blues and improvisational jazz, and Parsons was obviously inspired by country and blue grass.

While designing my books, I tried to echo that, best I could, by looking back into my own profession. By looking at who came before, such as book designers like Jan Tschichold, type designers like Baskerville and Bodoni, photographers like Ed Ruscha and Walker Evans. Whether people notice it or not, these books, in a graphic design sense, all pay homage to who came before. Not so much to bring back these times but to say, "Hey look, there was some really good work done in those days, let's build on it."

Dave: To throw your own question, in *Cucamonga*, back at you, what is it about the SoCal landscape that has spawned such eccentrics as Zappa, Beefheart, and Van Dyke Parks? Do you think there's some kind of unconventional thinking that proximity to the desert breeds? Or is it just random chance? Is there something special or different about these particular geniuses/eccentrics?

Rudy: Well, they're geniuses, which is what makes them special. They're able to express certain human qualities and draw inspiration from their surroundings better than most of us. It's interesting to note, also, that Parks and Parsons are not from California. Van Vliet is. But I'm sure that ultimately they all came here, or stayed here, because it's where most major record companies were situated in the 60s. So they did all live in and around Los Angeles, which must be one of the most unique (sub)urban areas in the world. It's where the ocean, mountains and desert meet. Geographically it's an awesome place. One thing is for sure. Whether you are the developer who spends thousands of dollars pulling Joshua trees out of the ground to make way for subdivisions, or the artist who draws inspiration from it, nobody can ignore these surroundings.

Dave: How did you do your photographic expeditions?

FAIRPLEX NARROW BOLD
NARROW BOOK
& NARROW BOOK ITALIC

Did you do scouting or research of sites first, or were these random drives? If the latter, how did you determine what routes you would take?

Rudy: Since *Song Cycle* is one of my most favorite albums ever, I have always paid much attention to Van Dyke Parks. He is such an interesting character. Not just a great musician, but a great philosopher of sorts, with a serious interest in California culture and history. Plus he's a living part of California culture and quite ubiquitous. He's a prolific musician. Even though little has been written about him he shows up in the biographies of many other artists, and I have always kept track of what was said about him, and what he himself has said in some of the interviews with him that I've read. And over the years, in my head, I sort of built my own piecemeal biography of him. Then upon my first visit to the Mojave desert and in particular the fringe communities around the edges of the desert, I was just so taken by the environment I knew I would be back with a big bag of film. My only problem was that I didn't know where to begin photographing. There was just too much to photograph. I had to narrow things down. So one day when I was listening to Parks's song "Palm Desert" I realized he was singing about an actual town called Palm Desert which is right there on the edge of the Mojave, just south of Palm Springs. And when I tried to figure out his rather cryptic lyrics, I realized he was singing about real estate development issues, mixed with his own experiences of living in L.A. I then found out, I think from reading Brian Wilson's bio, that he had actually written *Song Cycle* while living in Palm Desert for a few months. This is when my idea for this book started. I decided to go out and photograph Palm Desert. See what this place was all about. This allowed me to focus on a very specific subject, which was situated in an area I loved, while paying homage to one of my heroes. The route I took was roughly determined by the places Parks mentions in his lyrics. But I also photographed spots in L.A., like Brian Wilson's house in Laurel Canyon where Parks often hung out when he was collaborating with Wilson on *Smile*, which was done just before *Song Cycle* was made. With *Cucamonga* and *Joshua Tree* I roughly followed the same pattern.

Recently Van Dyke Parks took me on a tour of the locations and former locations of the major recording studios in L.A. like Gold Star, Sunset Sound, Western. They are all housed in rather generic looking stucco boxes without windows. But when I think what was created inside these boxes, it instills awe in me. Parks took me inside Sunset Sound, and to me that felt akin to walking into The Louvre for the first time. The walls of Sunset Sound are covered with gold and platinum records by bands I've listened to all my life. This whole West Coast/L.A. music scene in the late 60s and early 70s was a very special place and time, and in particular the role that Warner Bros. played in all this. A lot of faith and money was put in supporting rather unusual and non-commercial music. I'm really surprised there hasn't been a book published on the history of Warner Bros. Again, this is not just for nostalgic reasons. I think we could all learn something from it.

Anyway, during my short studio tour with Parks a little seed planted itself in my head. Gold Star, for instance, where Phil Spector developed his "Wall of Sound," and where Brian Wilson recorded many of his tracks for *Pet Sounds*, is no longer there. A mini mall has taken its place. No great surprise. But sad nonetheless. So I took some photographs. I'm sure they'll eventually find their way into some kind of book project.

To view pages from Rudy VanderLans's books *Palm Desert*, *Cucamonga* and *Joshua Tree*, and to view Zuzana Licko's Fairplex typeface family, please visit the Emigre website at www.emigre.com

OPPOSITE PAGE:
FAIRPLEX NARROW BOOK
WIDE BLACK
& WIDE MEDIUM

FAIRPLEX WIDE BOLD
& WIDE BOLD ITALIC

PAGE FROM AN IMAGINARY BOOK

Gold Star
Former Location at Santa Monica Blvd.
and Vine St., Hollywood, CA.

Design Firm: **EDWARD FELLA**, Valencia, CALIFORNIA (USA) Works: (LEFT) Ba

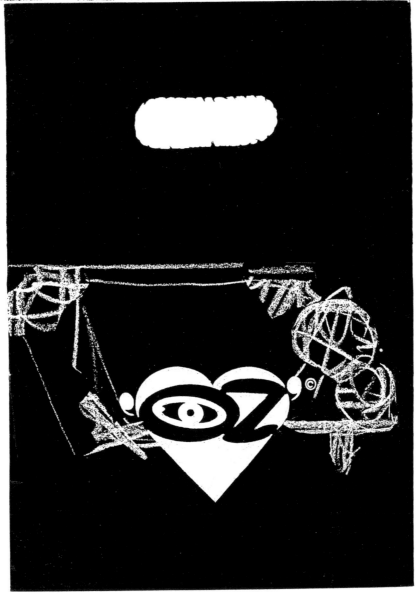

2002

f 1991 HOLiday GREETINGS PIECE – (RIGHT) Part from 2002 VISITING ARTIST LECTURE in AUSTRALIA   ART DIRECTION, DESIGN AND ILLUSTRATION: ED FELLA

LECTURES:
MICHAEL CLARK
ED FELLA
at
LOYOLA UNIVERSITY
"EAST COAST
meets
WEST COAST
on
THE GULF COAST"
THURSDAY
MARCH 14
7:02pm, 2002 A.D.
NUNEMAKER | AUDITORIUM
3rd FL, MONROE HALL
RECEPTION
FOLLOWING AT
AT THE DANNA
NEW ORLEANS AIGA

2002

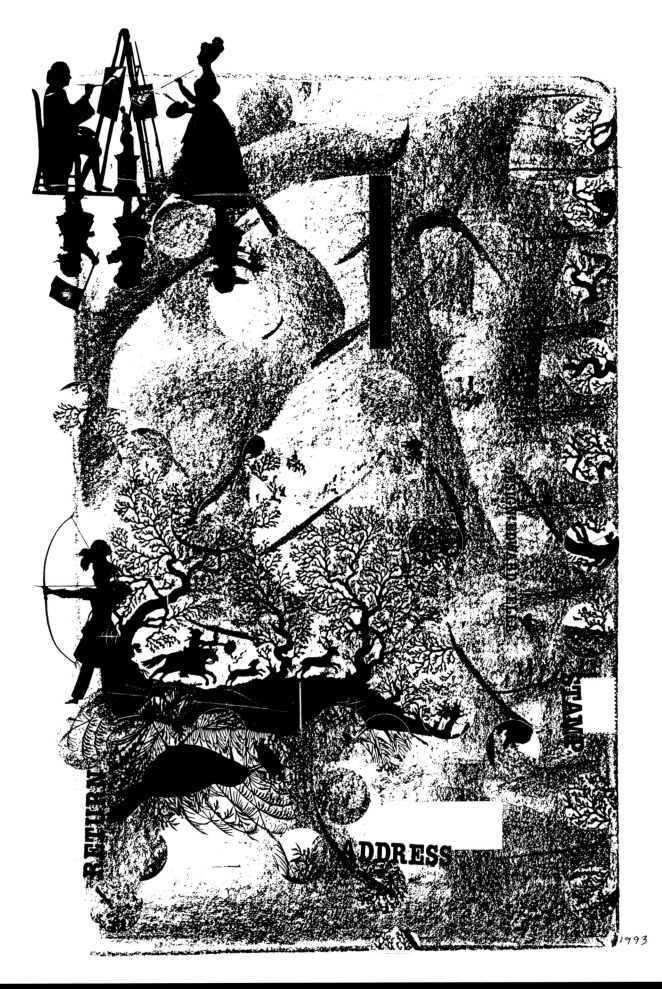

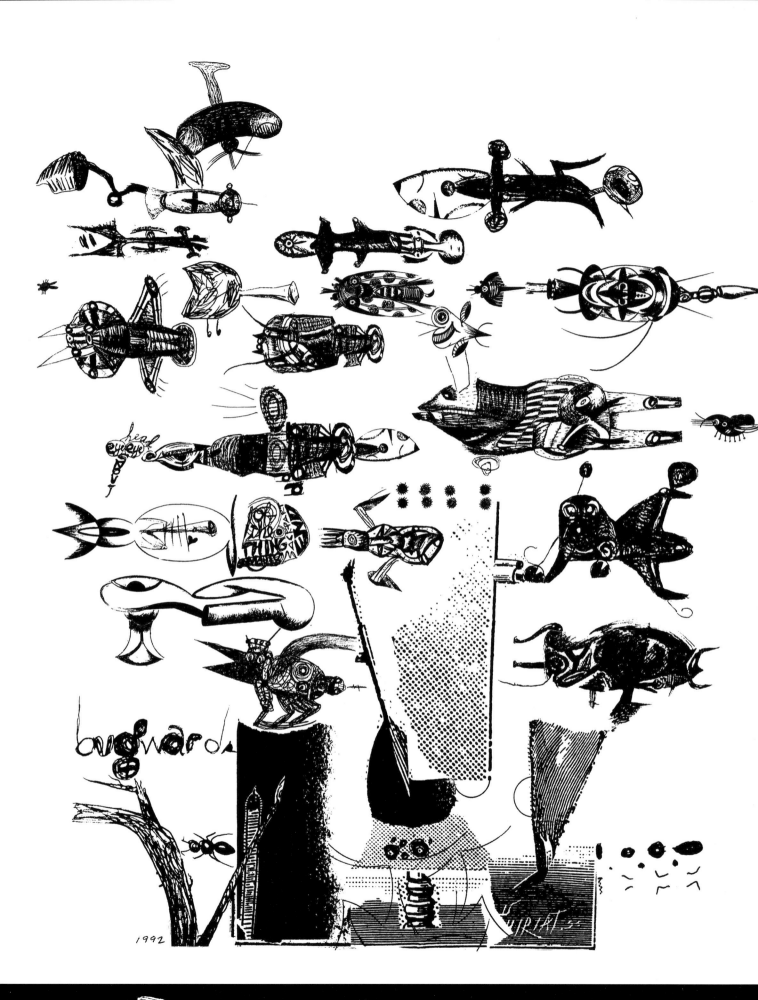

A LOGO LOW, JUST GO + LOW ANYTHING GOES = LOW GO NOWHERE LONG GONE DESIGN: EDWARD FELLA

—1999

VISITING DESIGNER ANNOUNCEMENT — (Right) Variations on Reverb Logo from Back of 1999 Announcement   ART DIRECTION, DESIGN AND ILLUSTRATION: EDWARD FELLA

Design Firm: Büro Dirk Rudolph, Bochum (Germany)
Works: Sono - 2000 Guns CD/12" Single - Polydor 2002   Art Direction and Design: Dirk Rudolph
Photography: Dirk Rudolph / Christof Schulte

Design Firm: Büro Dirk Rudolph, Bochum

Gail Swanlund

Design Firm: Gail Swanlund, Los Angeles

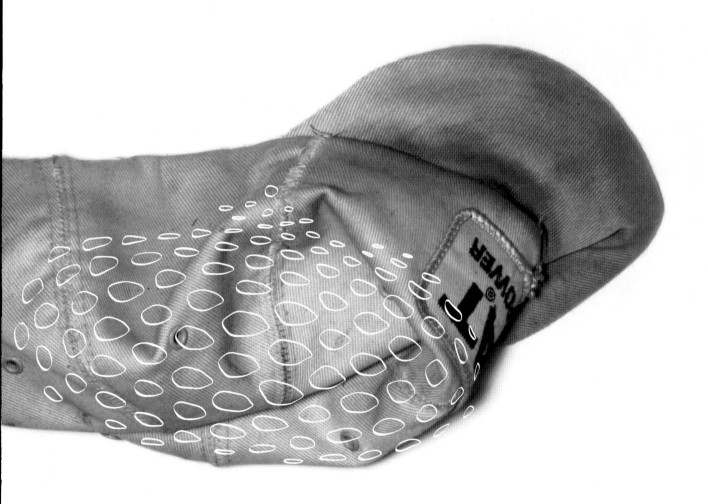

A (USA) Art Direction and Design: **GAIL Swanlund**   Photography: **SEAN DUNGAN (LOS ANGELES, Ca)**   Typefaces: **YUJU YEO**, Rebecca BURCH, ANDREA TiNNES

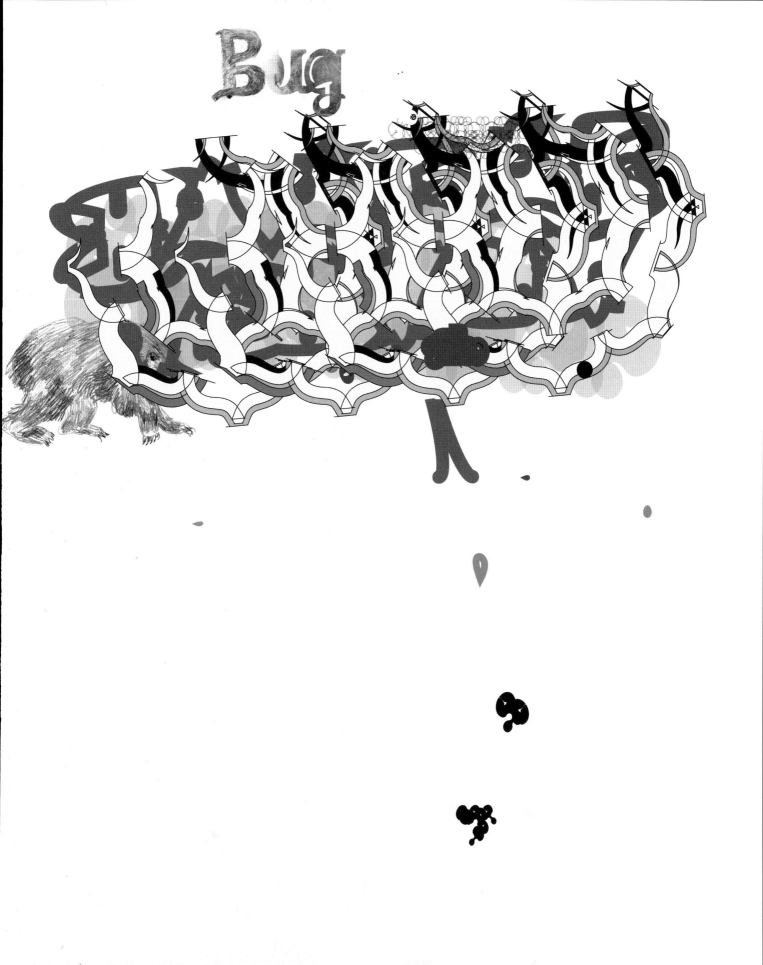

DESIGN FIRM: GAIL SWANLUND, LOS ANGELES, CA (USA) ART DIRECTION AND DESIGN: GAIL Swanlund
PHOTOGRAPHY: SEAN DUNGAN (LOS ANGELES, Ca)
TYPEFACES: YUJU YEO, Rebecca BURCH, ANDREA TINNES

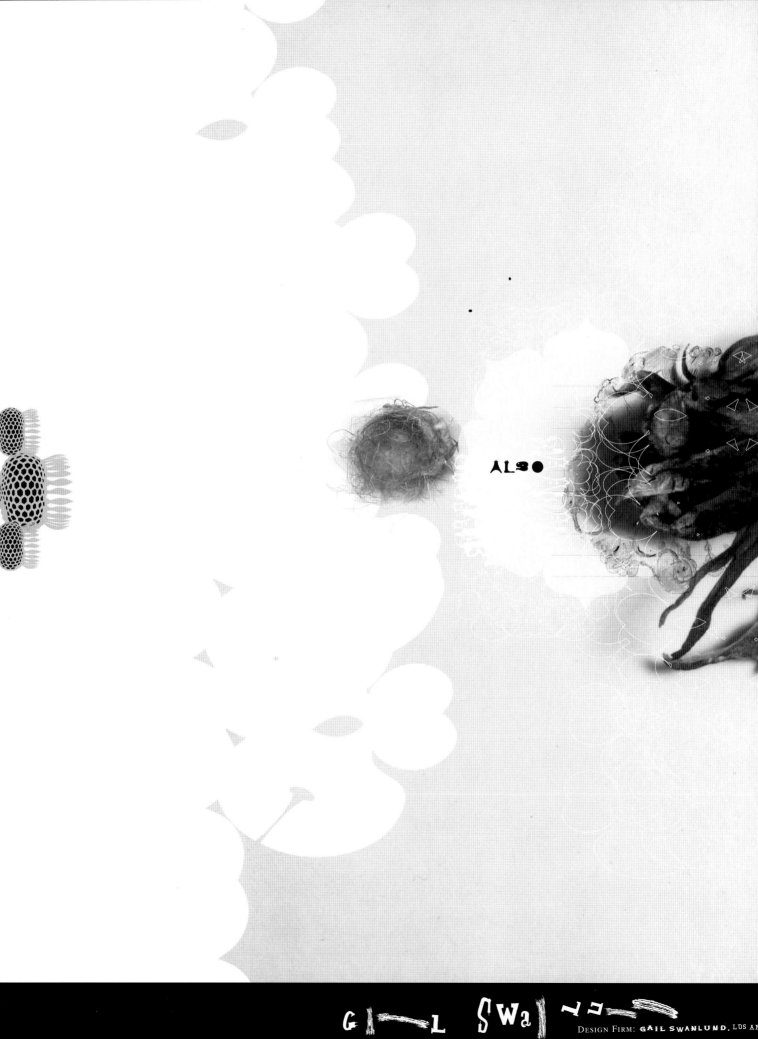

Design Firm: **WHY NOT ASSOCIATES**, London (UK)   Title: **Cursing Stone** and Reiver **Pavement, Carlisle**, England   Client: **Carlisle City** Council
Art Direction and Design: **WHY NOT ASSOCIATES** in collaboration with **GORDON YOUNG**   Photography: **Rocco Redondo**

DESIGN FIRM: WHY NOT ASSOCIATES, LONDON (UK)   TITLE: A FLOCK OF WORDS
ART DIRECTION AND DESIGN: WHY NOT ASSOCIATES IN COLLABORATION WITH GORM
PHOTOGRAPHY: WHY NOT ASSOCIATES

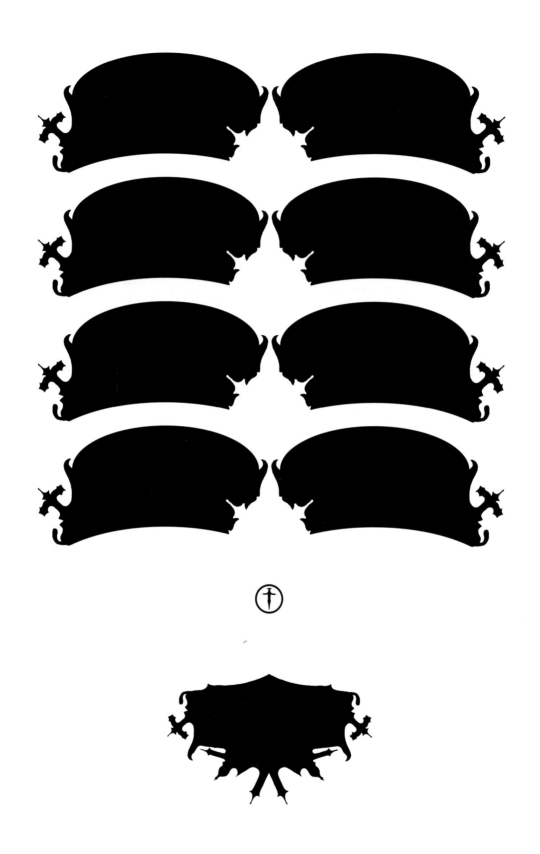

Design Firm: ANDREA LUGLI, Novi di Modena (Italy) Art Direction, Design & Illustration: ANDREA LUGLI

DESIGN FIRM: ANDREA LUGLI, Novi di Modena (Italy)   ART DIRECTION, DESIGN & ILLUSTRATION: ANDREA LUGLI

They were in his room now. She sat on a canvas camping-chair beside the chrome of his hospital bed, adjusted to face an architect on TV, ancient eyes welling with the struggle to put into words what it was like to witness one's vision swept away in scorn.

1.06 ■■ Jim, can you share your feelings, prodded the talk-show 'host,' dripping with understanding. Even without the sound, you'd be able to tell that this was the sensitive part of the show, the part before the audience turned on their 'guest.'

Functionalism once defined every skyline in the world, the architect said, gaining his composure. *Glass curtain walls hung like banners to 'ornament-as-crime,' 'individual signature-as-sentimentality' and 'romanticism-as-kitsch.' But now purity has given way to imitation medieval squares and faux space villages. Bread and circuses, circuses and bread and all because builders stopped giving the great unwashed masses what was good for them and started giving them,* bitter sarcasm came into his voice, *what they thought was good.*

The 'host's' face was a mask of empathy, easily readable though reduced as it was to the small scale of the screen—just as the Greeks wore exaggerated masks in their amphitheaters so that even the furthest (or dumbest) member of the audience could distinguish the tragic from the comic.

Close up on the host's cartoon sympathy. *I care....* pause for dramatic effect *about...your aesthetic.*

▲ groaned. *When the means and ends of the hoi polloi are given equal weight, equal time, equal volume as those of the intelligentsia, that is, when there is a true democracy of ideas, what becomes of culture? When the audience takes over the stage, what becomes of the playwright? What need is there for any art-ificer?*

«Would you like me to read?» ⓒ asked.

«No thanks.»

«Maybe your Tuesday treatment will be the one.»

«I don't give a damn about the treatment.»

«I do.»

«You give a damn about so many things that I don't.»

«Not so many. ▲»

1.07 ■ *Transvestites in the Modeling Industry....*
■ *Museum fund raisers increasingly turn from the black-tie cocktail party to walk-a-thons and other outdoor/heath-related events.*
■ *The Search for America's Sexist Lifeguards...*
■ *Cyberspace will redefine territory just as the invention of the clock redefined.*
■ *Gay teens call now! 1-900....*
■ *Gala means God is alive again and He's a she.*
■ *Grand Opera Meets Grand Ol' Oprey!....*
■ *Former CIA Director William Colby and former KGB Major General Oleg Kalugin collaborate to create the computer game Spy Craft...*
■ *Daughters' Disapproval of Mothers' Provocative Dress....*
■ *Monochrome ex-commies pouring onto the technicolor side of the Berlin Wall....*
■ *The BOFMOW (Based On Fact Movie Of the Week)...*

(BW) The morphing of *Grande Historie* into *petite histoires*, the morphing of paranoia into schizophrenia, the morphing of ambiguity into indeterminacy, transcendence into immanence, hierarchy to *jouissance*, 'less is more' to 'less is a bore,' mastercode to mass carnival, paradigm to hegemony, proletariat to cognitariat, words in print to image on screen, alienation to recess, genres to hybrids, writing to *archi-écriture*, artist priests to artist clowns, Logos to lacuna, sources to Ur text, criticism to Sur text, transparent window to self-conscious page, characters as mirrors on life to characters as tain of mirror; art mirroring life to life mirroring art to art mirroring art to mirrors mirroring mirrors mirroring...

He felt sorry for the ones who were left, the going but not yet gone, and what they had made to occupy themselves with until they went; novels that went loopity-loop or slogged through contemporary whines rendered in 19th century realism. Paintings that looked like cartoons. Music as a function of modern management. And the endless swarms of wanna bees full of buzz buzz buzz 'movie concept' buzz 'hypertext' buzz buzz 'Jacques Nietzsche' buzz buzz 'political art' buzz buzz buzz.... The educated artsy set. And the uneducated artsy set. Even the lowlies who emptied bed pans in this place wore gold chains and attitudes. It was the fashion tats that seemed most pathetic, though, for once the world turned back around to where only sailors and bikers got tattoos, the branded ones would wear their banality on their arms, ankles, backs and breasts as painfully as surgically attached love beads.

I'm getting as bored with dying as with everything else, he thought, realizing what he'd been thinking about.

«It's a bore,» he said out loud.

«What is, my dear?»

«Anything you do too bloody long.»

He looked at her, sitting between him and the glow of the television. It's gray-blue light shone on her pleasantly lined face and he could see that she was sleepy. The hyena made a noise just outside the window.

3.13
(BW)

«Do you feel anything strange?» he asked her.

«No. Just a little sleepy.»

«I do,» he said.

He had just felt death come by again.

(BW)

3.14 (BW) *Our nada who art in nada, nada be thy name. Thy kingdom nada, thy will be nada in nada as it is in nada.*

He told her how just in that instant he had felt like the old man in a story he had once written. For weeks on end, went the story, this old man stayed late into the night at the same cafe simply because he had no where else to go and the cafe was a clean, well-lighted and pleasant place to sit.

As ▲ spoke, a man emerged from the fluorescent white of the 24-hour Quickie Mart across the way. Styrofoam cup in hand, he got into the lot's one lone car and drove off. The two waiters in the story, ▲ continued, had to wait for this old man to finish nursing his brandy before they could close up and go home. So night after night one of the waiters, the young one, got more and more exasperated with this old man and his routine, his own life on hold sometimes until three in the morning. But the other waiter, the older one, understood that if they didn't stay open for the old man, there would be nothing but nada. Nada but the antiseptic chrome of steam pressure machines used in other bars, nada but those music-filled bars where it was impossible to stand with dignity, nada but the old man's own empty room, which is to say nada serving nada when everyones needed a place in which they could be at peace. A clean, well-lighted—

Suddenly, ▲ stopped talking.

Because, just then, death had come and rested its head on the chrome of his bed.

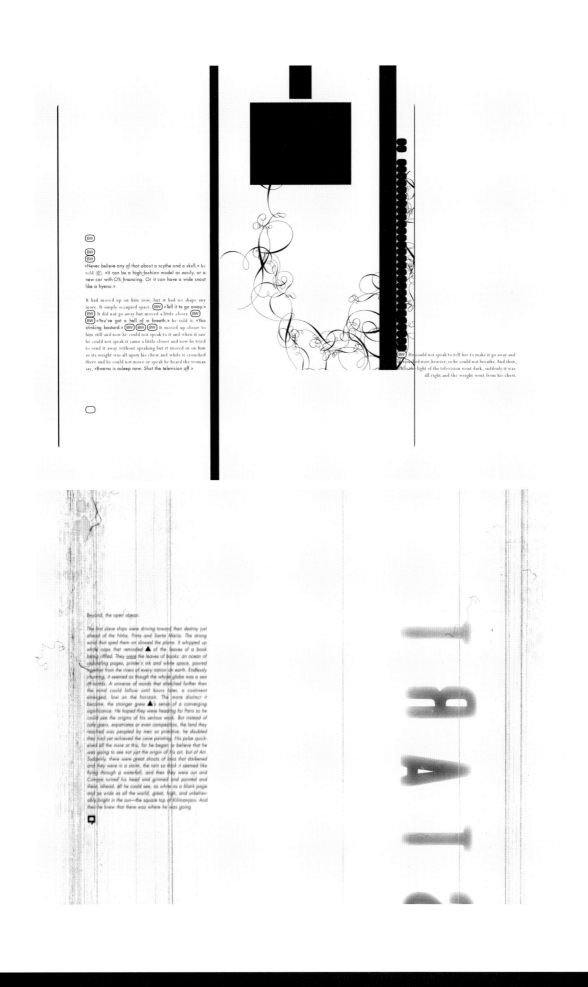

SUBJECT: **Farewell to Kilimanjaro (novella)** CREATIVE DIRECTION, ART DIRECTION, DESIGN AND ILLUSTRATION: **STEPHEN FARRELL**

A TRIP TO THE MUSEUM.

BEING THIRSTY.

MANIFEST OF MATERIALS:

PIANO ROLL,
NEW TYPE, NEW POEM,
CRANK, ROLLERS,
MOVIE APPARATUS,
A BUBBLE.

FRONT VIEW

WHERE

LANES

Y

SHAD-

COOL

GAZE,

MY

TO

PEARS

AP-

TURE

PIC-

A

WHAT

OH.

AND HIS WIFE.

A TRIP TO THE MUSEUM.

BEING THIRSTY.

SNAPPLE.

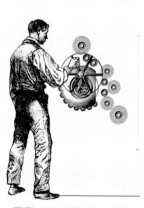

DESIGN FIRM: Stephen Farrell, SlipStudios (Chicago, USA)   SUBJECT: The Economy (installation proposal)   INSTALLATION & APPARATUS DESIGN, PROPOSAL: Stephe
TEXT: Daniel X. O'Neil   INSTALLATION SITE: Cooper-Hewitt National Design Museum   SUBJECT: LA SCRITTurA, LA MemoRIA MELiORE (MAgazine feature)   ART DIRECTION
TYPEFACE DESIGN: STEPHEN FARRELL   TEXTS: STEVE TOMasula & DANIEL X. O'NEIL   PUBLISHER: EmiGre

widely practiced by the time [he] began his training. THE DESIGNER OF Mss Folio BEGINS, THEN,
Cresci, like most of the masters [he] could have learned BY RUMMAGING THROUGH THE HANDWRITING OF THE DEAD,
from, would have worked out his alphabets with SEARCHING FOR A FORM THAT RESONATES. ONCE A
[intended] the family in mind. For the documentation DOCUMENT WAS FOUND, TOOLS OF THE CRAFT ENABLED THIS
hand used in the Uffizi registers, the goal was a rapid DESIGNER TO SYSTEMATICALLY ATOMIZE THE HAND AND ISOLATE
legible script: the characters were simplified so that ALLOWING THE RITUAL OF HANDWRITING TO PLAY OUT WITHIN
could be drawn with few pen lifts and without the acute CONFINED LATITUDE OF STANDARDIZED STROKES. DISSOLVED
ascension required of more calligraphic lettering. Beauty ARE THE TRACES OF FATIGUE VISIBLE IN AN UNEVENNESS OF THE
his alphabets on the oval, the designer worked out the ORIGINAL DAY'S LABOR. SO GOES THE CORPOREALITY OF THE
proportions of the part to the whole. He considered the MATERIALS, A QUILL, FOR EXAMPLE, RUNNING OUT OF INK
lyric effects of curved strokes versus singular connectors BEFORE LINE'S END. HYBRID CONFIGURATIONS OF SELECTED
the impression of forward motion in italic versus the LETTERS ARE ASSEMBLED, THEN DISSECTED TO CREATE
static posture of a vertical bar. In total, handwriting COLLAGES IN THE SHAPE OF % AND @ AND MANY OTHER
designers strove for SPREZZATURA, the elegant spectacle CHARACTERS [he] NEVER LEARNED TO FASHION. BY BRACKETING,
made to appear effortless. DECONSTRUCTING AND EMULATING, THE DESIGNER PLUCKS FROM
Elegance as effortless as a pen gliding across paper THE ORIGINAL TEMPO A RHYTHM AND CONTEMPORARY
Along with the shapes of letters, copybooks included ELEGANCE, AS EFFORTLESS AS TYPING. THE DESIGNER WHO
the order and direction of each stroke: a visual on-screen SPREZZATURA, an impression of effortless elegance.
memorize en route the [?] by drawing an informed stroke first and CREATES A NEW FONT USUALLY SIGNS A LICENSING AGREEMENT
[downward]; a copybook would also include direction WITH A FOUNDRY, THEN AWAITS KUDOS AND FINANCIAL REWARDS.
for shaping the pen, the posture for writing.... A clear WHAT USUALLY HAPPENS THOUGH IS THAT HIS OR HER FONT
like [?] would follow the models, practicing his spacing WILL BE BOOTLEGGED AFTER at even before THE INITIAL
and hand pressure, adjusting his speed so that shape PURCHASE, EARNING ITS CREATOR ABOUT 13 CENTS AS IT
specific shape and weight of his letters would adjust to CROSSES CONTINENTS AND OCEANS. EFFORTLESS AS
the needs of his specific writing task: obeisance upon COPY. TO THE CLICKING OF MICE, Mss Folio
time meant an embodiment of facts in the organic PROLIFERATES, THE FORM OF [A]'S HANDWRITING BECOMING
materials of [A]'s craft: the paper, the iron-gall ink, THE FORM OF OTHER POTENTIAL [A]'S WRITING ADS, WRITING
animal parts; an unconscious writing into existence of DOCUMENTS, WRITING POETRY, WRITING.... WRITING OUR
culture where facts were natural objects, likes names of CULTURE INTO EXISTENCE; OVER USERS OF THE FONT WHO
continents] waiting to be discovered. To write was to ARE SIMPLY AFTER "a look" ENACT THE FONT ITSELF,
inscribe for posterity a permanent record of weight and UNCONSCIOUSLY PERFORMING A REWRITING OF THE PAST INTO
measures [?] MANNER MORE SUITED TO THE PRESENT, A RECONFIGURATION
[?] KNOWLEDGE, AESTHETICS, READING, OR WRITING A SENSE OF
of scientific discovery OF HISTORY... WHICH IN OUR MOMENT IS TO WRITE,
No. 1492 COPYCOPY COLUMBUS NAVIGO L'OCEANO AZZURO [IF] HE NO LONGER DISCOVERS A NEW WORLD.

We now know that 2000 men were killed in those few days in Srebrenica, 200 years and five hundred miles from the list of the dead in Florence. But there is no list of the dead—of Srebrenica, and the list of the missing is not good enough.

It is fitting and right that someone would take this typeface and use it to talk back at Europe with a reflective, terrified glance. For those of us who write in English today, the craggy lips of the Romantic languages look back at us each time we see our own words—.

With this typeface and a computer anyone can compose a document in the deliberate image of those who have gone before in dignified civility. That is what I do now, in my hand, in this typeface—demand a list of the dead from those who killed them.

Dal Xoul

DESIGN AND ILLUSTRATION: Stephen Farrell and Jiwon Son

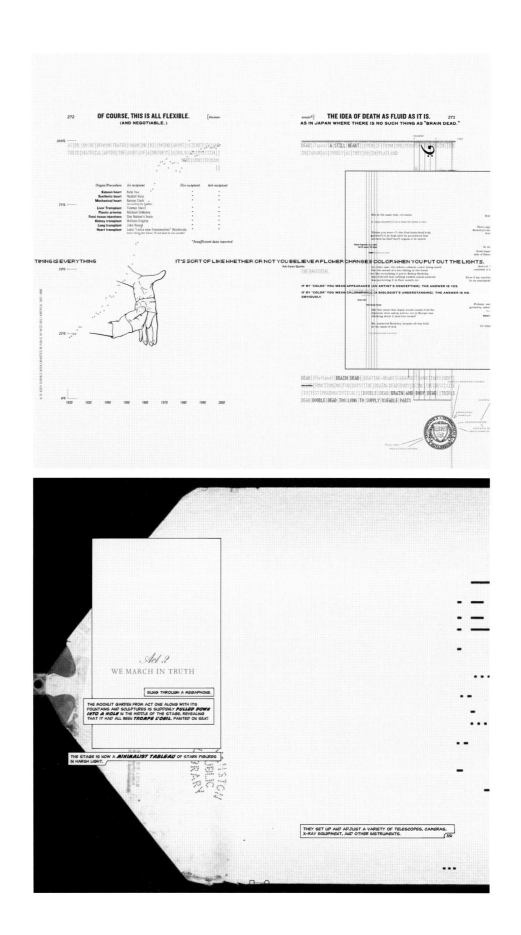

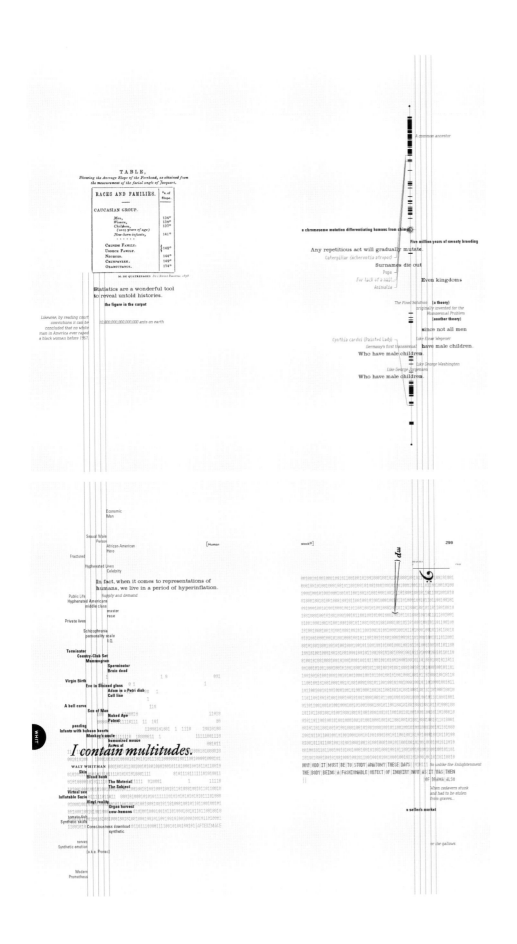

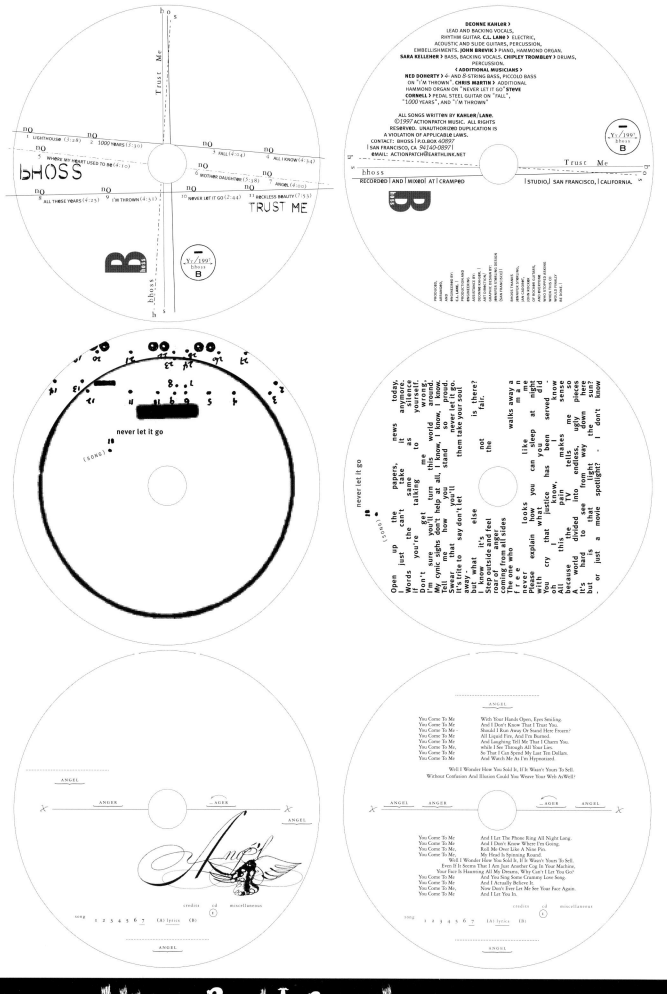

MOTHER DAUGHTER

She wrote me a note on the day I was born.
Seen as a fish laying torn.
Bursting from water, gasping for breath.
Peering at tiny distinctions.
Feeling peculiar and somehow misplaced.
Wondering how someone
that mad shaped my face.

She wrote me a note of suicide on the day I was born.
Seen as a fish with its flesh laying torn.
Bursting from water, gasping for breath, peering at tiny distinctions.
Feeling peculiar and somehow misplaced,
wondering how someone that mad shared my face.
Hurtful and good, a messenger to me,
  a witness and a lover.
Why am I still standing here?
  When will the truth kiss me awake?
    Wondering who you and I are, together.
      Whispering your name as I break.
        Rushing to find my own answer,
          rendered with sticks in the sand.
          Reaching for ghosts that I know I can't own.
          Wreckage that falls from my hand.
        I began as they all do,
        with fumbling and heat.
          As soon as we met you admitted defeat.
          Troubling simile, rapturous attention,
          too much for one to contain.
        You're the night clerk
          of my emotional hotel.
        Others come and go as you ring
        that slow knell,
          steady like iron, watchful like mother,
          true as so many prescriptions.

6
Now that it's over I follow her down,
laying my cheek on the dark, loose ground.
Pulling me towards her as the music begins,
  she croons in my ear that I am her twin.
    Struggling with the earth,
both above and below,
my limbs pull apart,
and planted,
will grow.

Song 5

You told m^e that I'd b^e
  the one to chang^e your mind.
You said that w^e'd b^e tog^{e}ther until the ^{e}nd of tim^e.
I soon found out that your id^{e}a of tog^{e}ther isn't min^e.
I swallowed my pride, I f^{e}ll in lov^e, and I took my plac^e in lin^e.
I n^{e}v^{e}r b^{e}li^{e}v^{e}d that I'd b^e the one l^{e}ft standing still.
L^{e}ft to wond^{e}r wh^{e}n it was this turn^{e}d surr^{e}al.
My fri^{e}nds t^{e}ll m^e to l^{e}t it go,
  and c^{u}t my loss^{e}s now.
But th^{e}y
  don't know
    the you I know,
      the on^e
    I can't l^{e}t go.
Ev^{e}ry day I f^e^{e}l the sting of you insid^e.
  I bow to this ic^e wh^{e}r^e my h^{e}art us^{e}d to b^e.
To return to you would only b^e a failing of my will,
  but my m^{e}mori^{e}s just tortur^e m^e. I'll l^{e}arn to g^{e}t by.
It s^e^{e}ms that it is ^{e}asier to scorn you
  in the dark, than drop my sham^e,
    shout out your nam^e,
      com^e into light and conf^{e}ss.

Lying here all by myself,
  I think of you and what we felt,
    and I wonder where you are today.
But that's okay,
  'cause I don't miss you anyway,
    in fact I rarely cry, when I hear your name.
It makes me sick
  to see you leaving me so easily,
    y o u   actually asked me can
     w e   b e   f r i e n d s ?
Like I'd pretend that all my lust for you had
gone away?
Still you can't say why you don't feel the
                                    same.

This unreciprocated yearning
was never meant to live a lengthy life,
  and so I close the door.
                          But just so you know,
you've mistaken   m e for
someone
        e   l   s   e
       S   o   m   e   o n e
who'd rather die   than be alone.
I'm thrown.

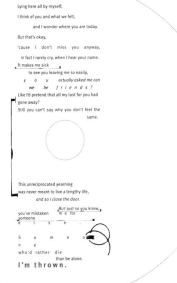

M: JENNIFER STERling Design, SAN FRANCISCO (USA)
ILLUSTRATION: JenNifer Sterling
PHOTOGRAPHY: JoHN CASado
WRITER: DEONNe KaHLER

JeNNIFer STerLInG

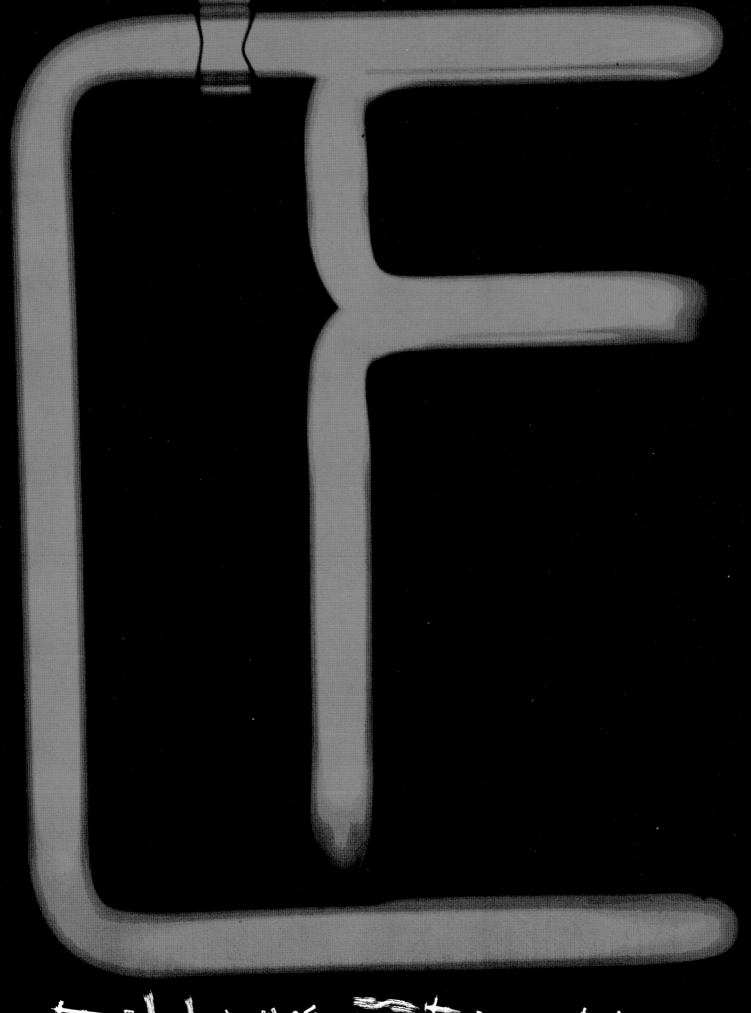

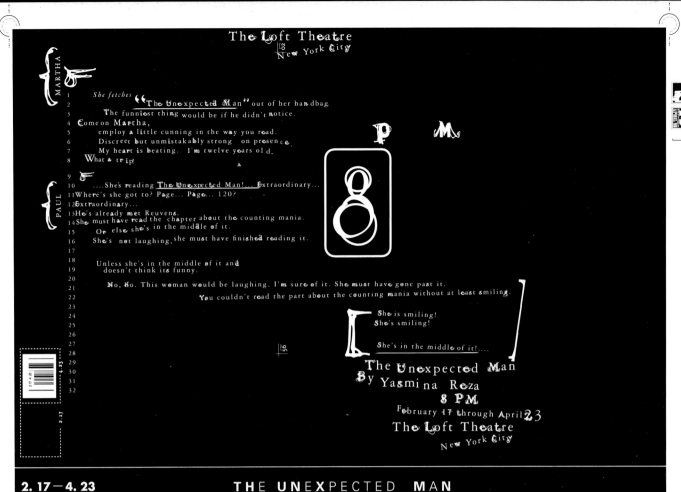

Lou Reed features a self portrait with embossed type on its cover. The lyrics are divided into chapters according to each album. Every album has its own typographic style reflecting the overall mood and feel of the words and the music. The steadiness and simplicity of his work is reflected by the use of one single typeface throughout the book. This typeface gets drunk, does drugs, becomes incomprehensible, dresses up, is mean, visionary, gorgeous and glowing. Its Lou's voice.

CLIENT: STEFAN SAgmeister ART DIRECTION: STEFAN SagmeistEr DESIGN: STEFAN SagmeisTER, Hjalti Karlsson, JAN Wilker PHOTOGRAPHY: Lou REED YEAR: 2000

SAGMEISTER

STEFU SAGMEISTER

Design Firm: SAGMEISTER Inc. NY (USA) Subject: Sagmeister INC. Business CARDS.
Art Direction: Stefan SAGMEISTER Design: Stefan SagmeisTER
Client: SAGMEISTER INC. Year: 1998

STEFAN

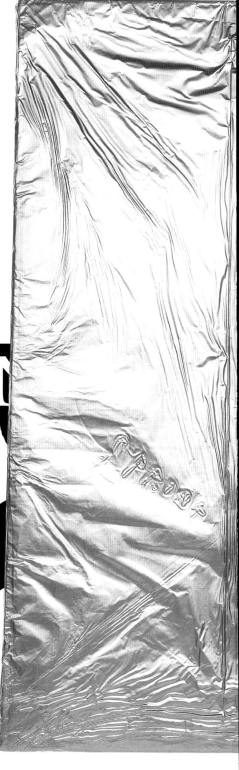

SAGMEISTER

DESIGN FIRM: SAGMEISTER Inc. NY (USA) SUBJECT: AnNi KUan CATALOGUE

SUBJECT: ANNI KUAN

SUBJECT: Anni KUAn BusiNesS CA

Anni Kuan catalogue Alu (silver).
Spring/Summer 2001 fashion brochure for New York fashion designer Anni Kuan featuring rather personal stories about the designer printed on fresh newsprint and wrapped in crisp aluminum foil.

Anni Kuan Business Card.
Anni Kuan is an Asian fashion designer working in New York.
On the business card different abstract elements come together to form the distinctive Anni Kuan logo mark.

Art Direction: Stefan Sagmeister   Design and Copywriting: Joshua Gurrie   Client: Anni Kuan   Date: 2001   Size: 16 x 23 inch, 410 x 585 mm
Catalogue Alu (silver).   Art Direction, Design and Copywriting: Stefan Sagmeister   Client: Anni Kuan   Date: 2000   Size: 16 x 23 inch, 410 x 585 mm
Concept: Stefan Sagmeister   Design: Stefan Sagmeister and Hjalti Karlsson   Client: Anni Kuan   Date: 1998   Size: 3 1/2 x 2", 90 x 50 mm

67

Sundial Postcard.
With a couple of simple folds, the viewer can turn this card into a working sundial.
This card was just printed in a limited run of 2000 for our studio as a self promotion. The sundial gives the correct time anywhere in the U.S.

DESIGN FIRM: Sagmeister Inc. NY (USA)   SUBJECT: Sundial POSTCARD.   CONCEPT: Stefan Sagmeister   DESIGN: Stefan Sagmeister and Veronica Oh

Design Firm: MAROK, LODOWN, BERLIN (Germany) Work: 'Destroy THE Pattern' Art Direction, Design and Illustration: MAROK

SOME WILL FIGHT ON THEIR FEET TO INSURE THAT OTHERS DO NOT HAVE TO LIVE ON THEIR KNEES

剣道
喰首

問字は一時の恥

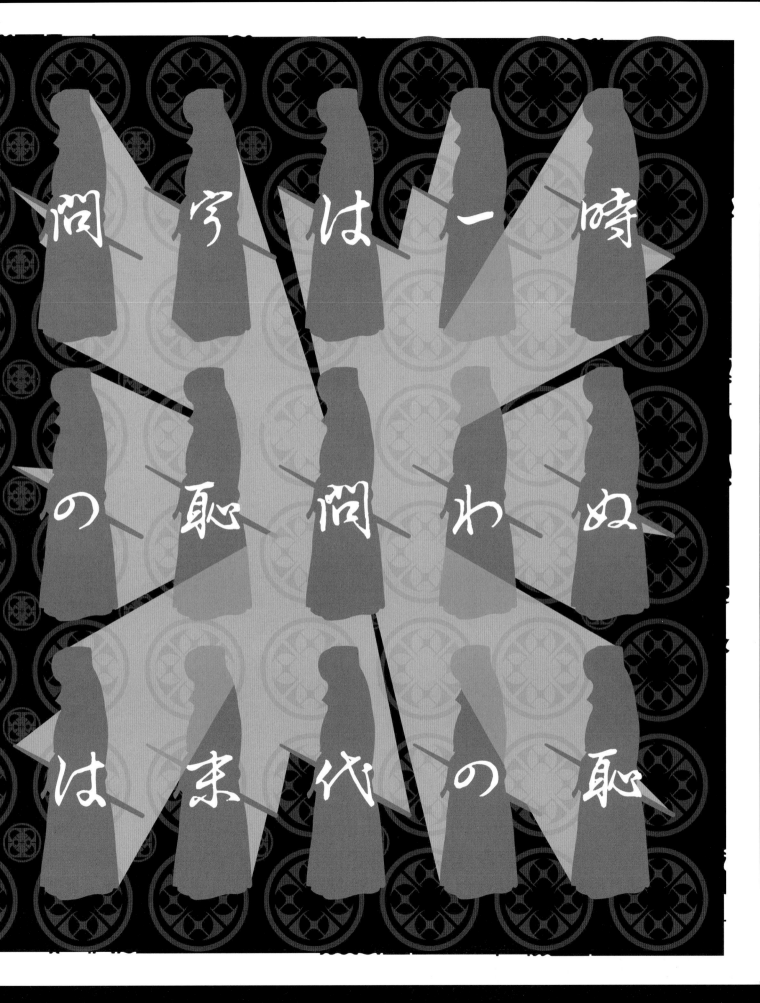

Roberto Bagatti

DESIGN FIRM: ROBERTO BAGATTI, MILAN (ITALY) CALLIGRAPHY: TOMONORI TOYOFUKU ART DIRECTION, DESIGN AND ILLUSTRATION: ROBERTO BAGATTI

Design Firm: HAUSGRAFIK, Zürich. Client: REITSCHULE BERN Work: Poster for the Concert of TAV FALCO and the Panterburns 2002
Art Direction, Design and Illustration: URS ALTHAUS

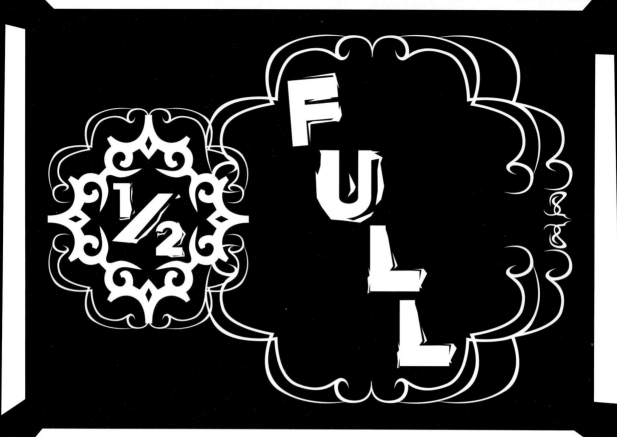
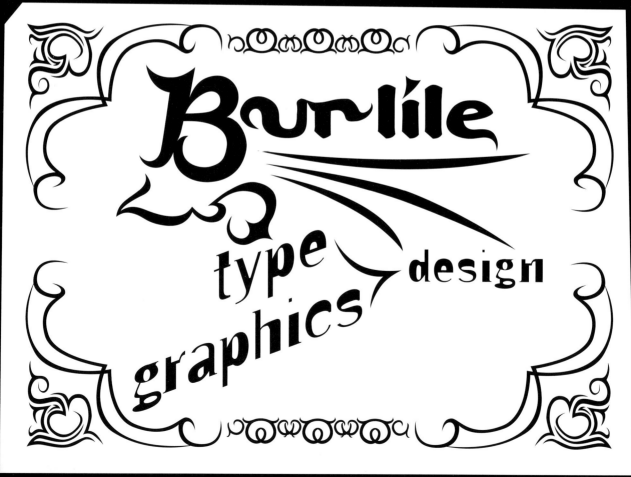

DESIGN FIRM: MARCUS BURLILE

LILYIN WANTED™

ATANDABCDEFGHIJK
LMNOPQRSTUVWX
YZabcdefghijklm
nopqrstuvwxyz12
34567890?!-R--C-W
qhFRTAiTMq pg•adR
ÆNO.%/o$:¢Œ.&()[]...

ATANDABCDEFGHIJK
LMNOPQRSTUVWX
YZabcdefghijklm
nopqrstuvwxyz12
34567890?!@©ßgh
fwd0/0iTMyhq•d±Æ
NO.%/o$:¢Œ.5()[]...

LILYIN™

LILYIN SAGUARO™

ABCDEFGHIJKLM
NOPQRSTUVWXY
ZABCDEFGHIJKLM
NOPQRSTUVWXYZ
NO.1234567890 AT
¨¨!?<>_+=-(){}$¢%\
:;()ªº/≈÷TM£•ZŒAÆ
◊Ø()ñ:-—¸¡AND...

LILYIN Tupelo™

ABCDEFGHIJKLM
NOPQRSTUVWXYZ
abcdefghijklmnop
qrstuvwxyz123456
7890AT&!?$¢*-=+i¿
o§No.M®©™¨:'4(){}\'
()ŒØAND Æë No.hYß
çGFÇ;µE THE ØÁÅ()ªº

LILYIN TARNISH™

ABCDEFGHIJKL
MNOPQRSTUV
WXYZ&ABCDEFG
HiJKLMNOPQRSTUVWXYZ12345
67890AT!?ŠČ'=+i¿H-WNO.□B©™.Qii
[]Ω..)ŒAND Æ Gb43C÷ dfÇ/2OAEL...

Fonts by Burlile **Sold by Plazm**

PLAZM A sampling of black and white pages from PLAZM Magazine issues 1 - 12 www.plazm.com

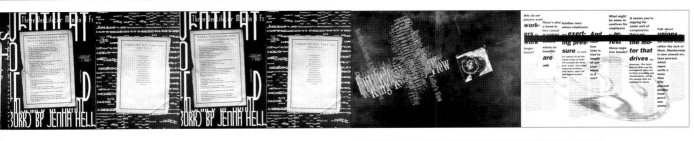
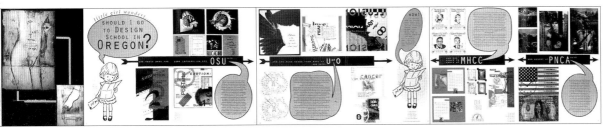

nd, OR, (USA) ART DIRECTION: JOSHUA BERGER DESIGN: JOSHUA BERGER, Tomomi ARITA

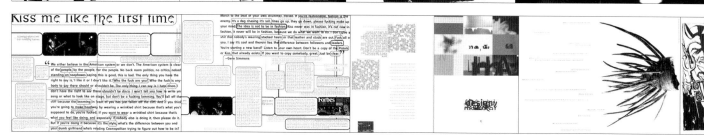

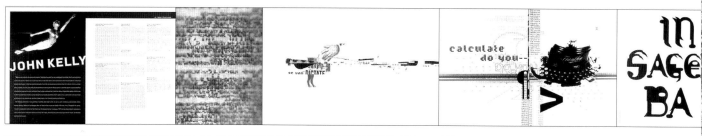

PLAZM A sampling of black and white pages from PLAZM Magazine issues 13 – 26   www.plazm.com

DESIGN FIRM: **PLAZM**, PORTLand, OR, (USA)

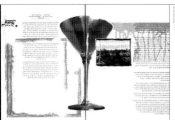

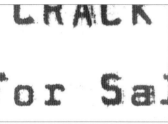
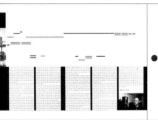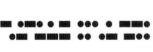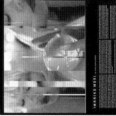
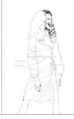

DIRECTION: JOSHUA BERGER   DESIGN: JOSHUA BERGER, Tomomi ARITA

PLAZM presented at the aiga 2002 voice conference : words sarah dougher : see live version at www.plazm.com

In visual language, signs can be silencers as easily as they can be catalysts. Our work as designers and artists is to motivate signs to do our work of meaning. This seems like an easy enough concept for the post structuralist world.

But the ability of sign to shift meanings, and our right to shift that meaning, is essential as we watch the destructive cultural banality of patriotism flood our visual landscape.

The screeching eagle swoops down onto the lot full of new cars. The theater lines stretch out as people file in to see regurgitated scenes of the Viet Nam War, the Second World War, any war. Children are compelled daily to celebrate a nation that neglects to feed and educate them properly, neglects them at a rate parallel only to the race for vengeance and warmongering. Women are insulted by our government which refuses to uphold their right to equal pay for equal work, yet admonishes the fundametalists of the world, suddenly able to identify "oppression" based on gender.

These ironies are as numerous as they are depressing and repetitive. They flash before us like all the flag bumper stickers—singular in their symbology, motivated by our fellow designers to sell everything from cars to fleece parkas. To what end? Brand loyalty?

DEAN KARR

DESIGN FIRM: DEAN KARR
CLIENT: Nothing / Interscope

tichrist Superstar PROMOTIONALS, 1996, NEW ORLEANS, Lousiana   CLIENT: Nothing / Interscope   PHOTOGRAPHY: DEAN KARR

Design Firm: **Dean Karr - The Mine**, Los Angeles (USA)   Work: **Marilyn Manson**'s Antichrist Sup

WORK: **MARILYN MANSON**'s Antichrist Superstar PROMOTIONALS, 1996, NEW ORLEANS, Lousiana   DESIGN FIRM: **DEAN KARR - THE MINE**, Los Angeles   CLIENT: **Nothing / Interscope**   PHOTOGRAPHY: **DEAN KARR**

DESIGN FIRM: **DEAN KARR - THE MINE**, Lo
CLIENT: **Nothing / Interscope** PHOTOGRAP

Work: **MARILYN MANSON's Antichrist Superstar** PROMOTIONALS, 1996, NEW ORLEANS, Louisiana

DESIGN FIRM: **DEAN KARR - THE MINE**, Los Angeles (USA) WORK: **MARILYN MANSON's** Antichrist Su

Tour PROMOTIONALS, 1996, NEW ORLEANS, Lousiana   CLIENT: **Nothing / Interscope**   PHOTOGRAPHY: **DEAN KARR**

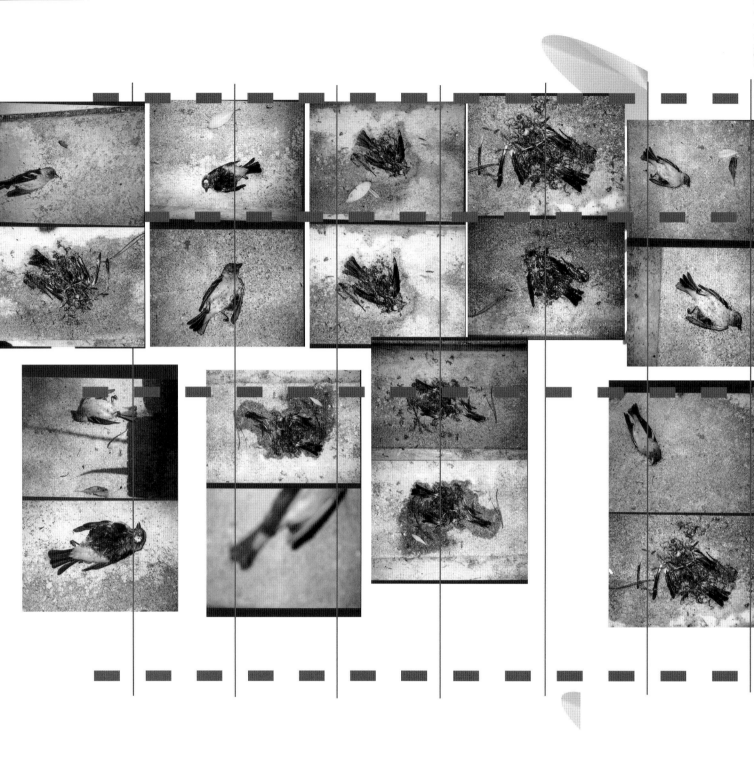

GENERAL WORKING GROUP

Design Firm: GENERAL WORK
Creative Direction, Art Direc

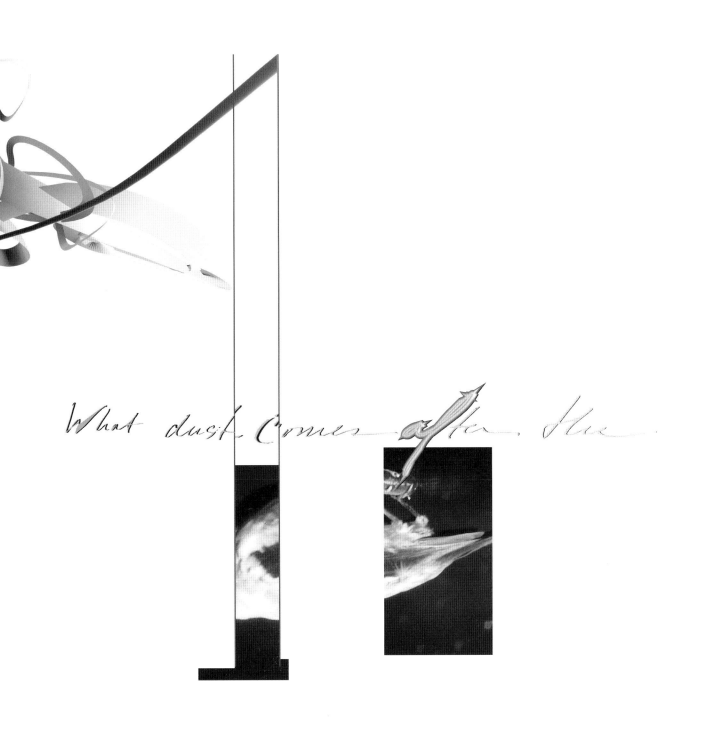

GENERAL WORKING GROUP

DESIGN FIRM: GENERAL WORKING GROUP, SAN FRANCISCO {USA}   CREATIVE DIRECTION, ART DIRECTION, DESIGN, PHOTO AND ILLUSTRATION: GEOFF KAPLAN

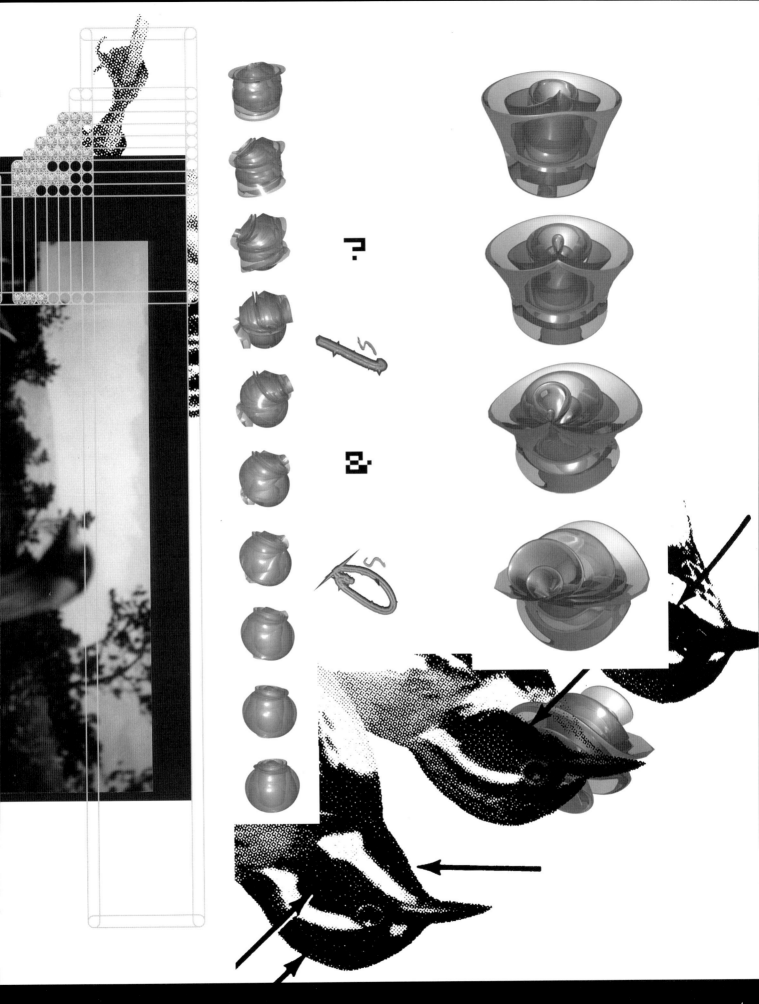

project: Page2

DESIGN FIRM: HANDGUN (PORTLAND, OREGON – MINNEAPOLIS, MINNESOTA) CLIENT: EBON BOND
ART DIRECTION: DAVID ZACK CUSTER DESIGN: DAVID ZACK CUSTER COPYWRITER: EBON BOND
ILLUSTRATION: DAVID ZACK CUSTER

project: 1424 26thth St. W

project: CZR

DESIGN FIRM: HANDGUN (PORTLAND, OREGON - MINNEAPOLIS, Minnesota
CLIENT: CZR (LEFT) AND DAVID ZACK CUSTER/HANDGUN (right)   CREATIVE DIRECTION: DAVID ZACK CUSTER
ART DIRECTION: DAVID ZACK CUSTER   DESIGN: DAVID ZACK CUSTER   COPY: DAVID ZACK CUSTER
ILLUSTRATION: DAVID ZACK CUSTER

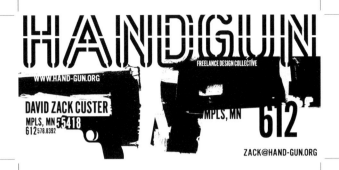

project: HandGun

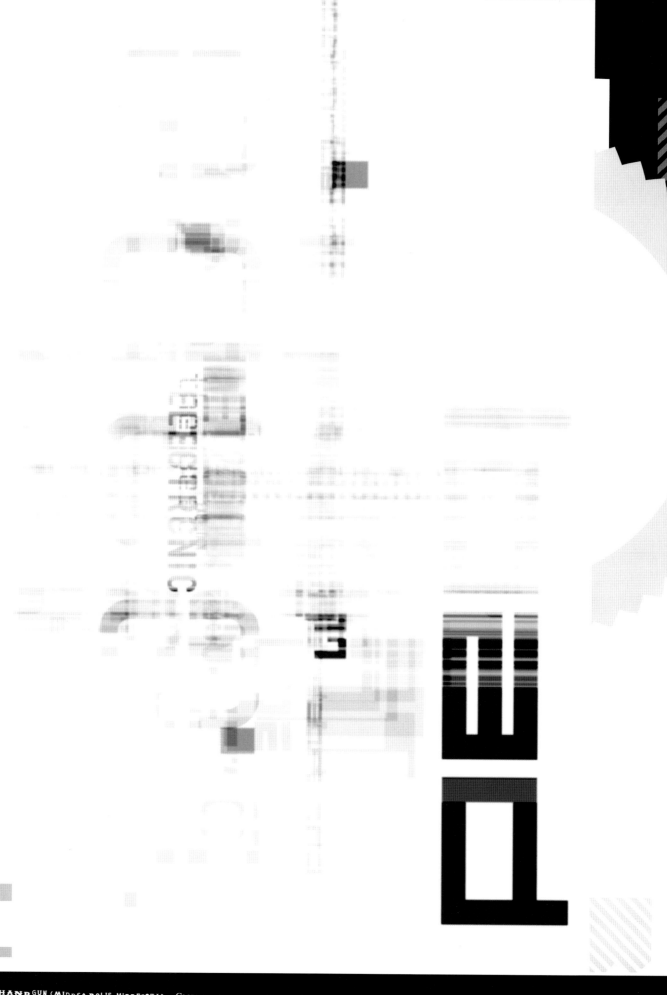

Design Firm: **HAND**GUN (Minneapolis, Minnesota) Client: **Minnesota Electronic Theatre** Creative Direction: **David Zack Custer** Art Direction: **David Zack C**
Illustration: **David Zack Custer**

project: Minnesota Electronic Theatre

THE PREJUDICES AGAINST THIS CO/ LOR ARE STILL SUF/ FICIENTLY STRONG TO REQUIRE A DIS/ CUSSION OF THE PROPERTIES OF BLACK AND A VIG/ OROUS DEFENSE OF ITS MANY VIRTUES. BLANKET DENUN/ CIATION OF A CO/ LOR COMPLETELY IGNORES THE RE/ LATIVE NATURE OF ANY COLOR OR FORM.

DESIGN FIRM: FRANK HEINE, U.O.R.G., Stuttgart, GERmany CLIENT: U.O.R.G. ART DIRECTION AND DESIGN: Frank Heine TYPEFACE DESI

White space, is of course, always with us. The problem now is what we can make it mean. Can we rescue it from the class ridden value it has been overloaded with in QUALITY design? Can white space be used in such a way that it is outside the burgeois/Modern aesthetic? The key is in understanding what white space signifies. If white space remains in the Modern code we are simply reproducing an appropriated formula; a code of commercial system of design, despite its inbuilt change, modification, innovation, asymmetry, etc.

[Das 3. Beispiel ist unkonventionell, aber gut.]

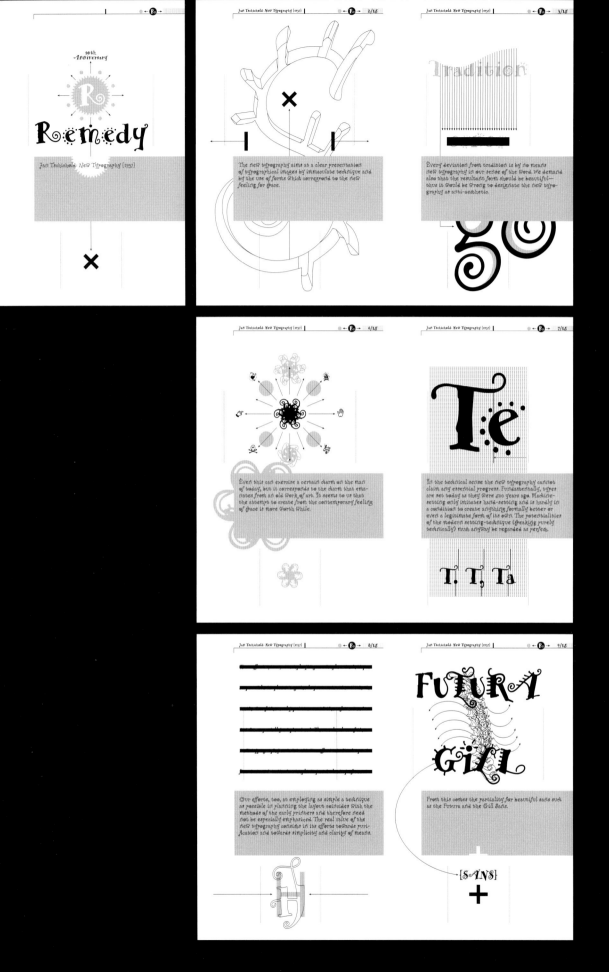

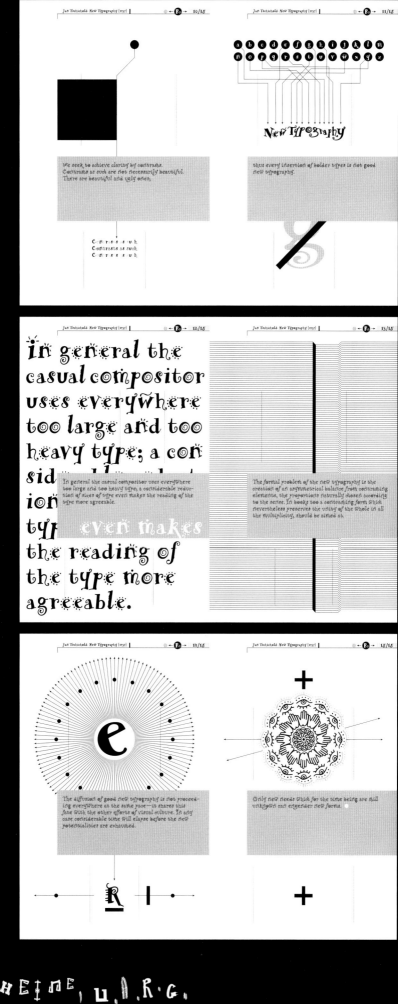

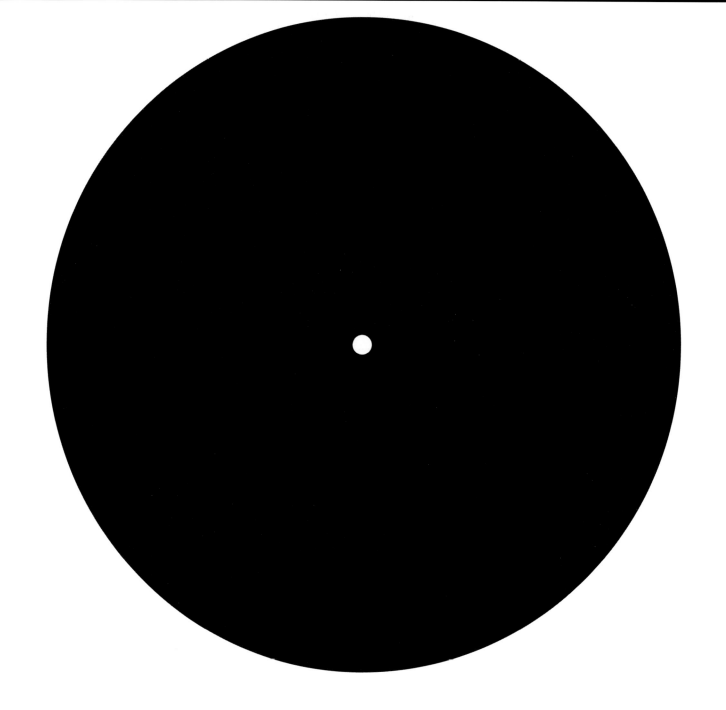

1. Reihe: **Seltene Platten**
Samstags 14 Uhr
19. 2. 2000 Bruce Haak, The Electric Luzifer, 1968 Moog Sounds
26. 2. 2000 Silver Apples Spectrum, Spaceman 3

Labor für Soziale und Ästhetische Entwicklung
Berger Kirche, Bergerstrasse Ecke Wallstrasse, Düsseldorf
In Zusammenarbeit mit Hitsville

2. Reihe: **Got it?**

Freie Reden mit christlichem Unterton

Thorsten Nolting

Montag bis Freitag 18. Februar bis 31. März

15 Uhr Nachdenklich

16 Uhr Bei der Arbeit

17 Uhr Im Getümmel

18 Uhr Natürlich

Plakat: **Fons M. Hickmann**

Labor für soziale und ästhetische Entwicklung

Berger Kirche, Bergerstrasse Ecke Wallstrasse, Düsseldorf

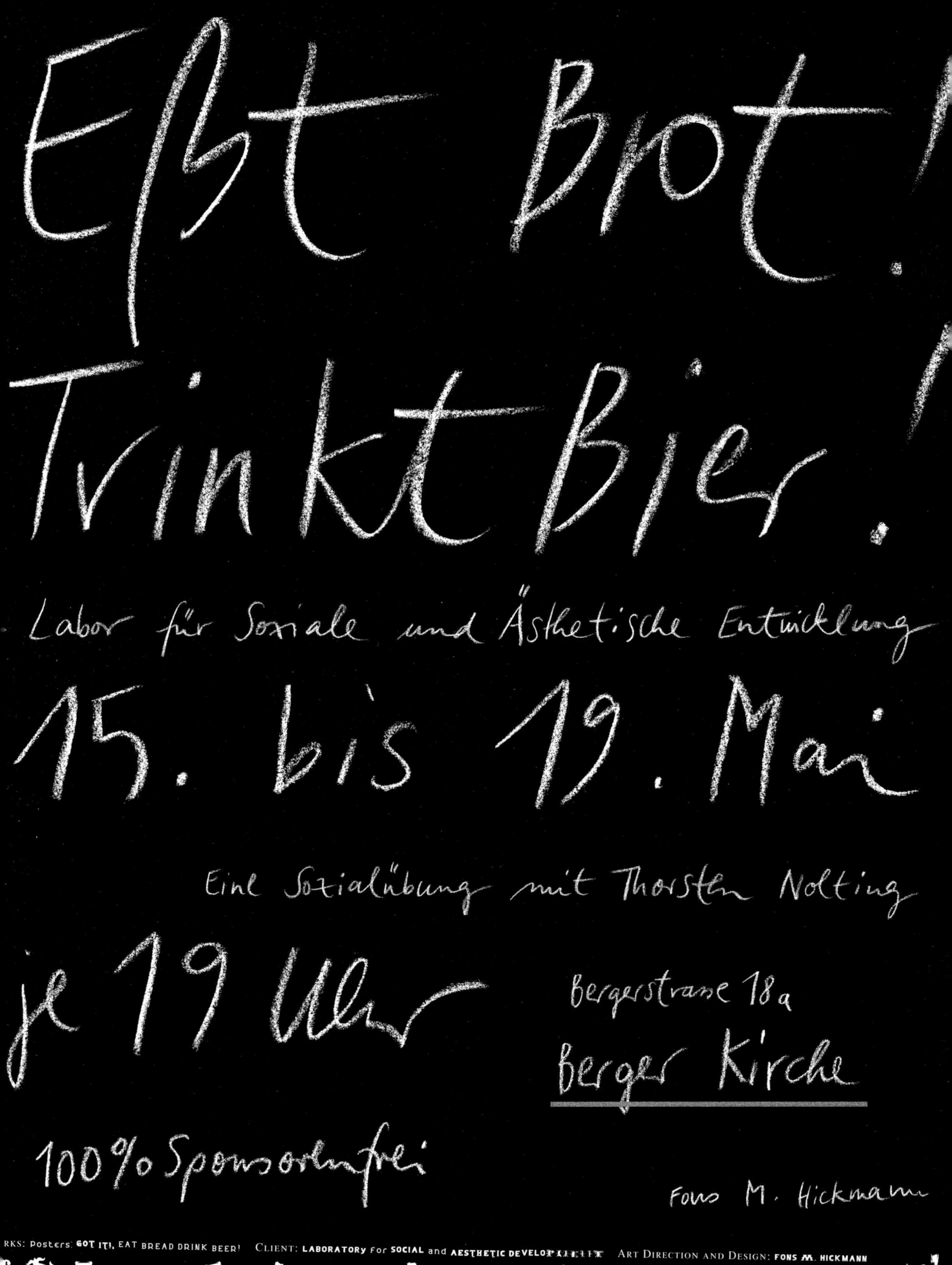

Eßt Brot! Trinkt Bier!

Labor für Soziale und Ästhetische Entwicklung

15. bis 19. Mai

Eine Sozialübung mit Thorsten Nolting

je 19 Uhr

Bergerstraße 18a
Berger Kirche

100% Sponsorenfrei

Fons M. Hickmann

Labor für
Soziale und
Ästhetische
Entwicklung

15.9.-29.9.2000

Altkleidersammlung und Verkauf
Montags bis Freitgs
15 bis 18 Uhr

Berger Kirche
Wallstrasse
Düsseldorf

DESIGN FIRM: **FONS MATTHIAS HICKMANN, M29, BERLIN**   WORKS: **POSTERS**. SECOND HAND. **HAVE AN ACIS BATH**   CLIENT: **LABORATORY FOR SOCI**

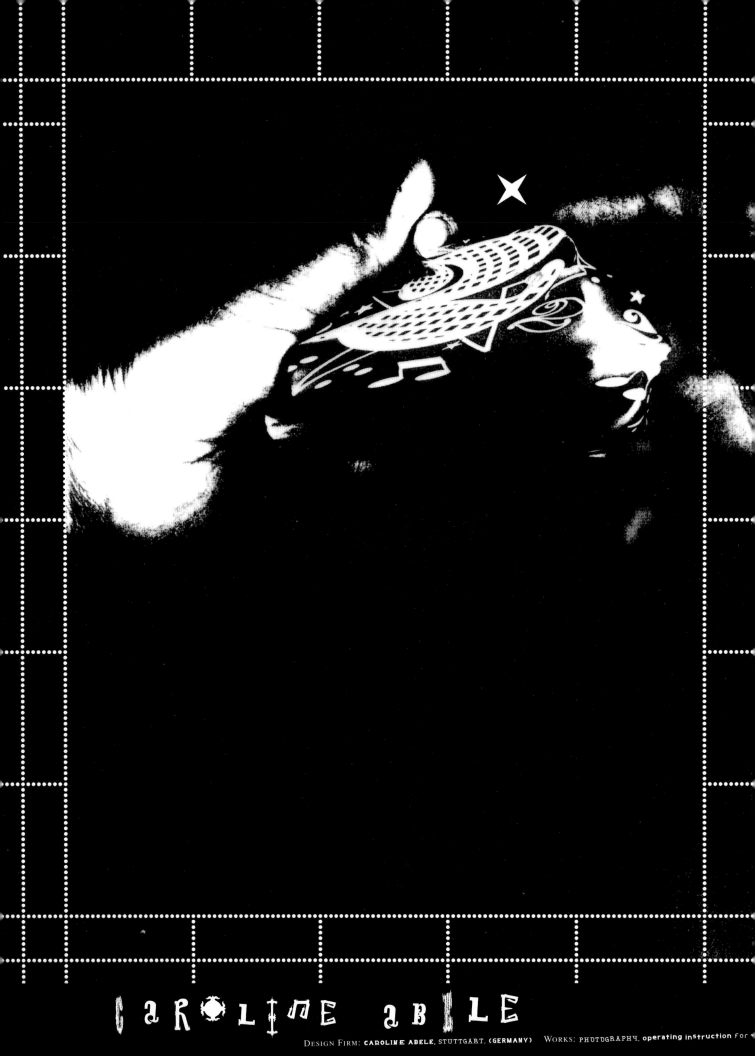

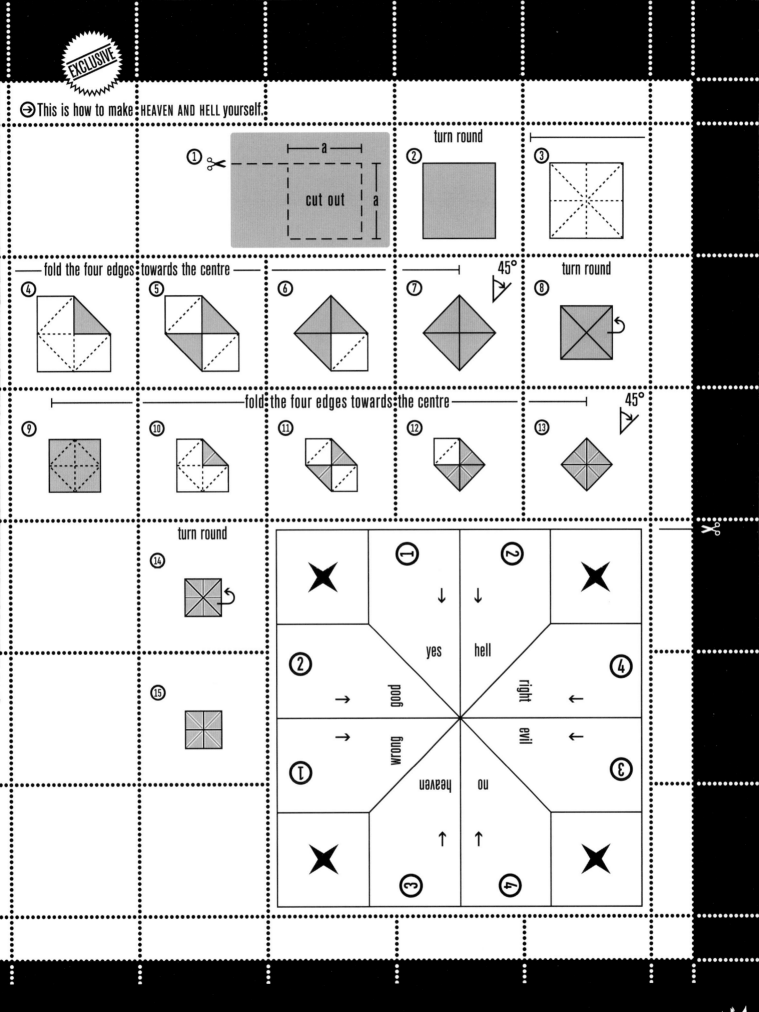

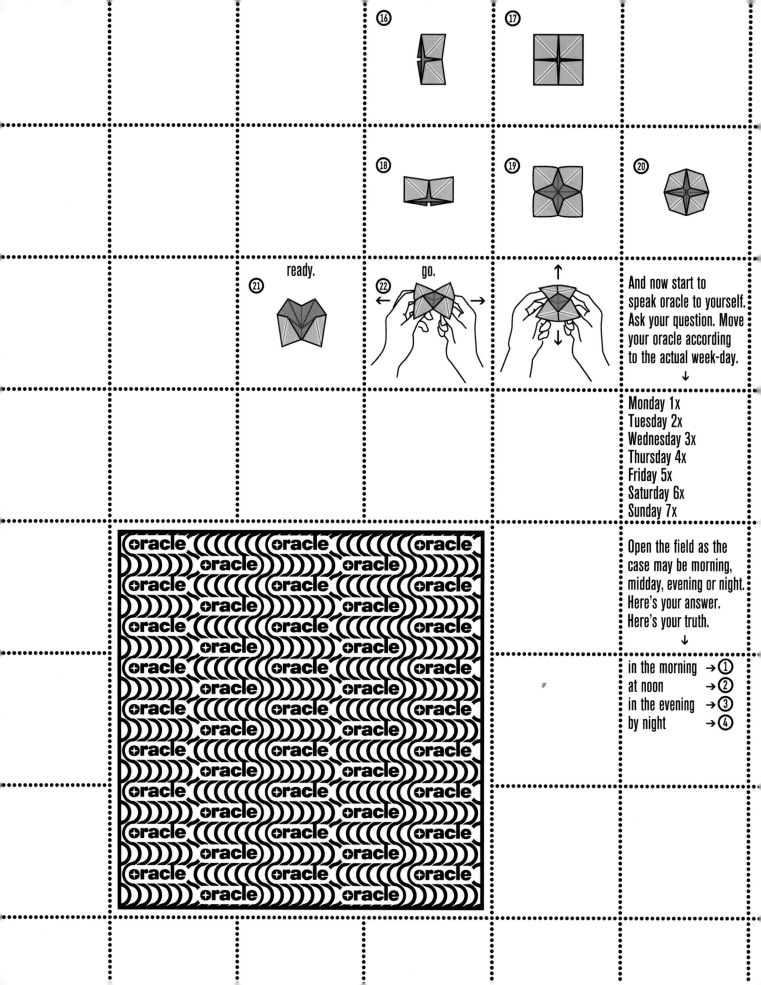

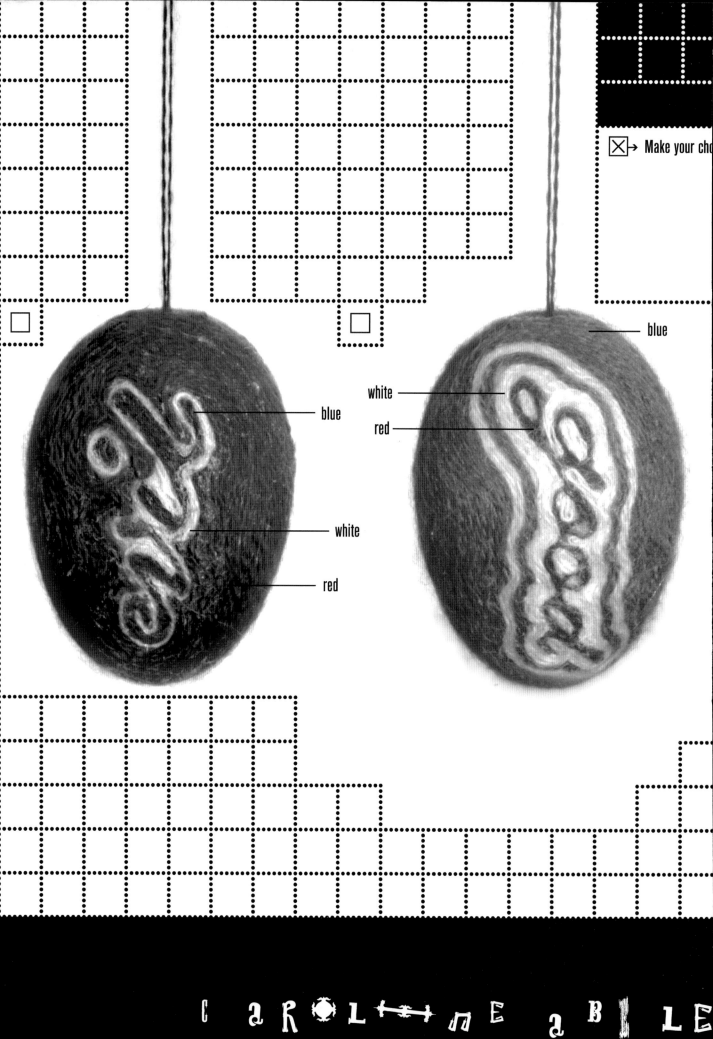

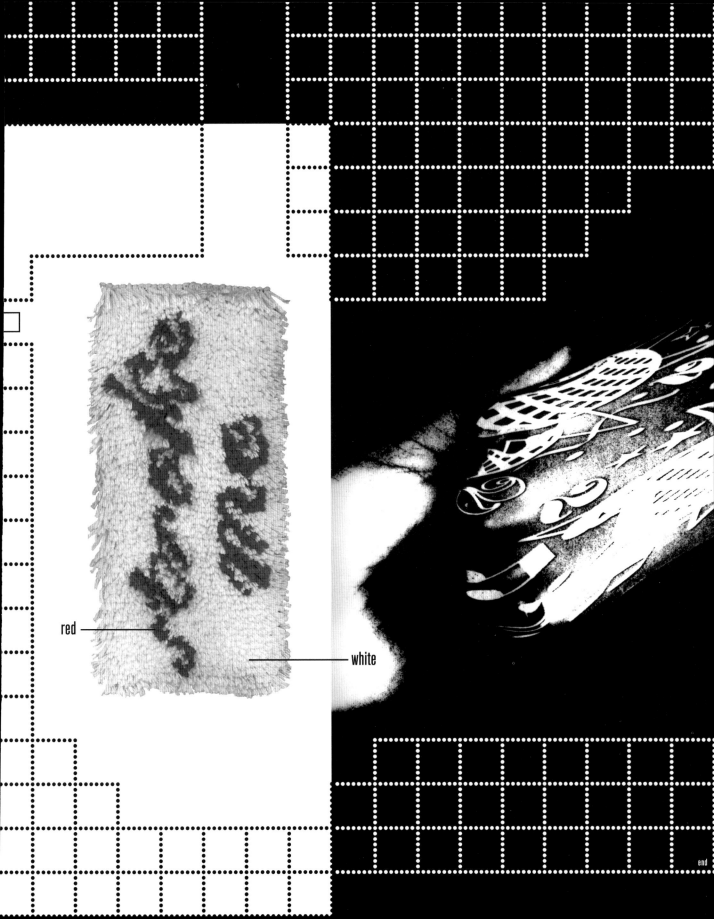

RNARI Advertising DEPT. - Civitanova MarCHE, ITALY. ART DIRECTION, DESIGN AND ILLUSTRATION: RAFFAELE PRIMITIVO

(FORMARI ADV. DEPT.)

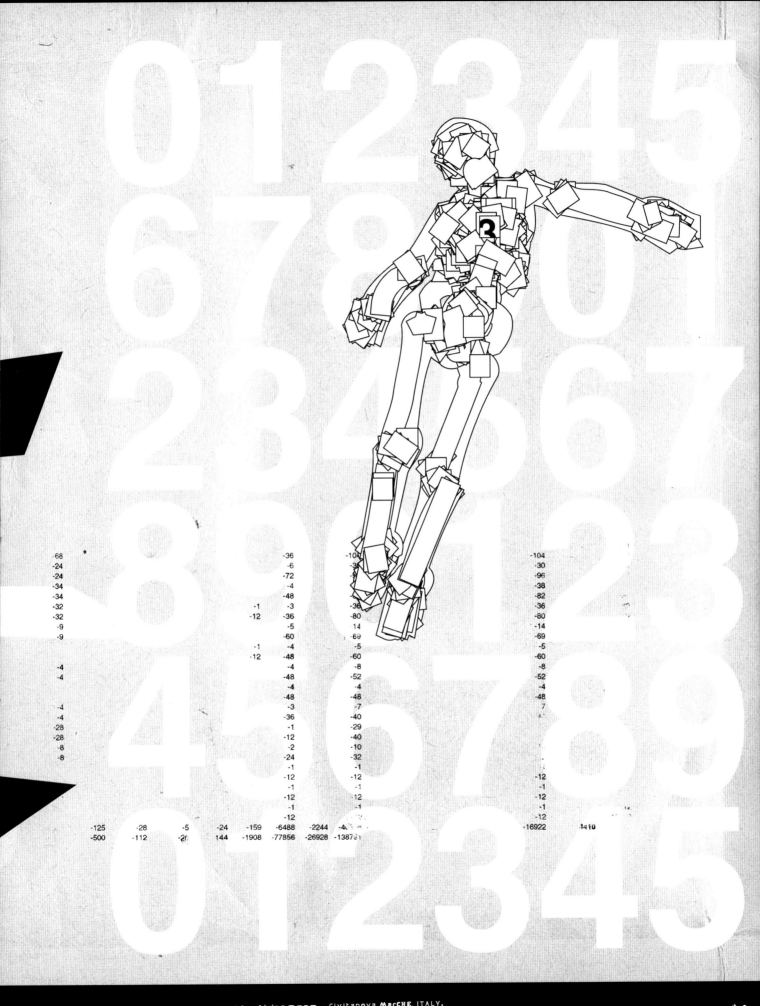

DESIGN FIRM: RAFFAELE PRIMITIVO, FORNARI Advertising DEPT.

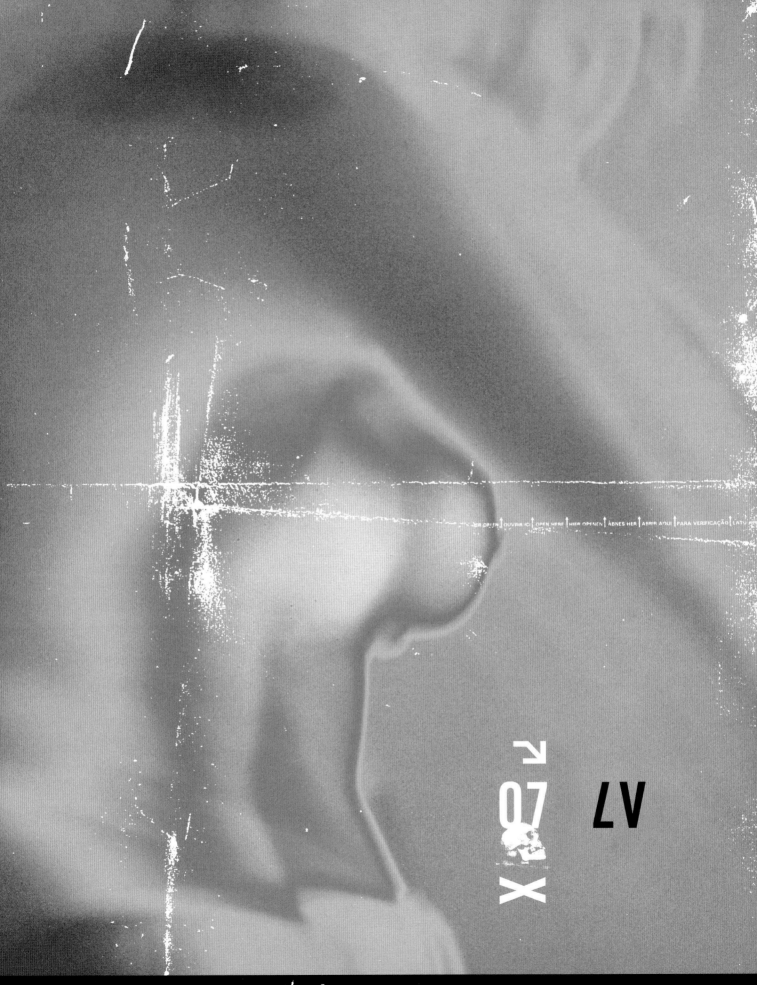

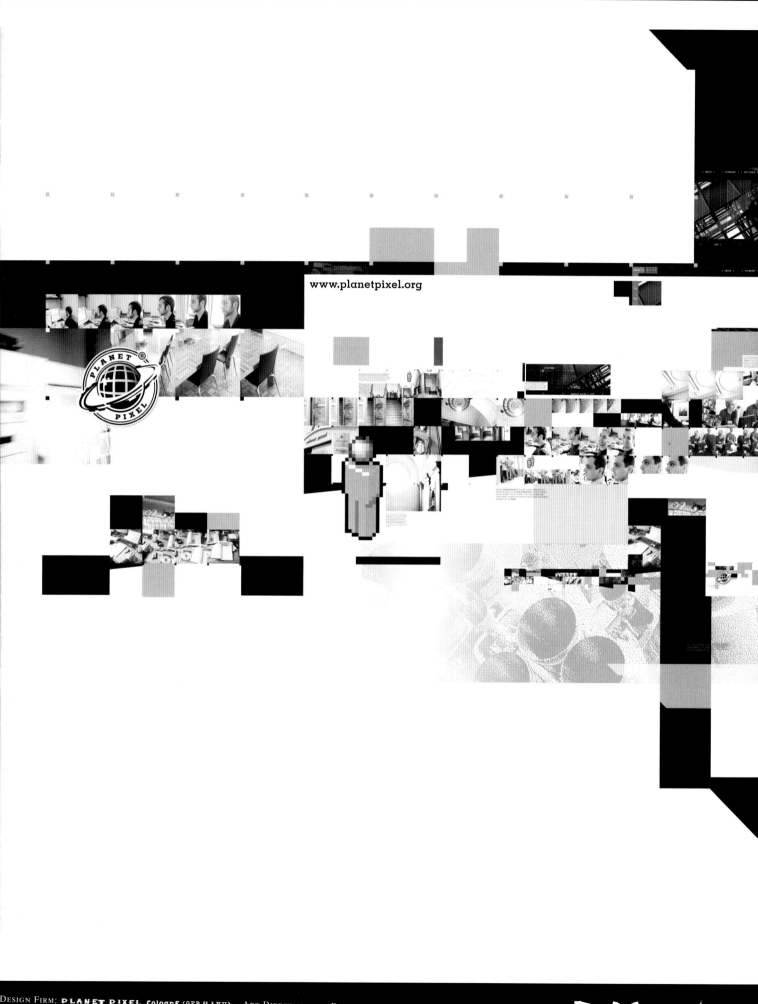

Design Firm: **Planet Pixel**, Cologne (Germany)   Art Direction and Design: **Anja Wuelfing**
Photo: **Anja Wuelfing, Oliver Funke**   Illustration: **Anja Wuelfing**
3D: **Ralf Essert**

BE

  Design Firm: **Planet Pixel**, Cologne (Germany) Art

NICE.

PLANET PIXEL
COLOGNE
GERMANY
WWW.PLANETPIXEL.ORG

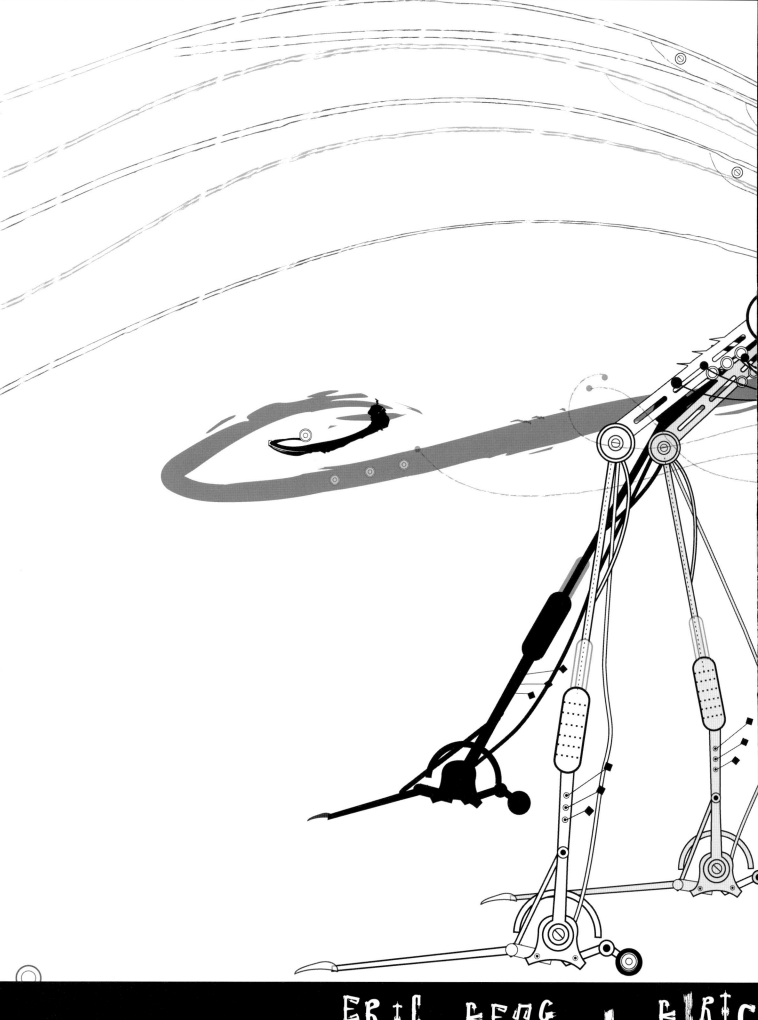

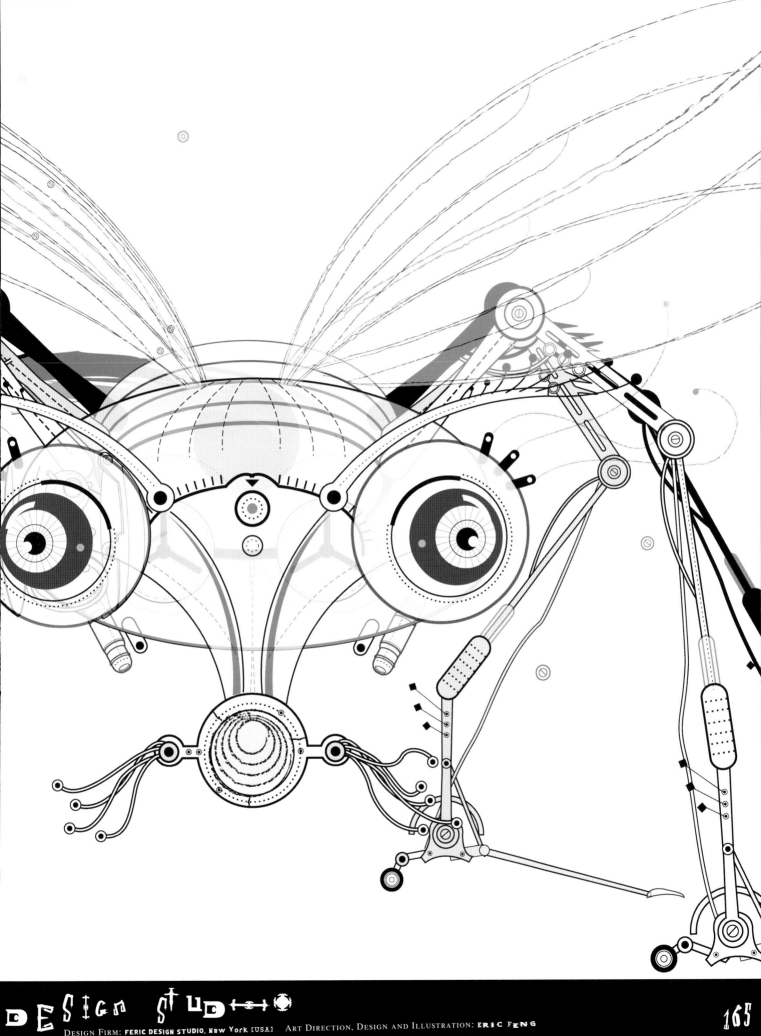

DESIGN STUDIO
DESIGN FIRM: FERIC DESIGN STUDIO, NEW YORK [USA] ART DIRECTION, DESIGN AND ILLUSTRATION: ERIC FENG

Design Firm: FERIC DESIGN STUDIO, New York [USA]   Art Direction, Design and Illustration: ERIC FENG

Design Firm: GESINE GROTRIAN-STEINWEG, ILLUSTRATION, BERLIN   Works: TRiP-ARt   Art Direction, Design and Illustration: GESINE GROtriAN-SteiNWEG

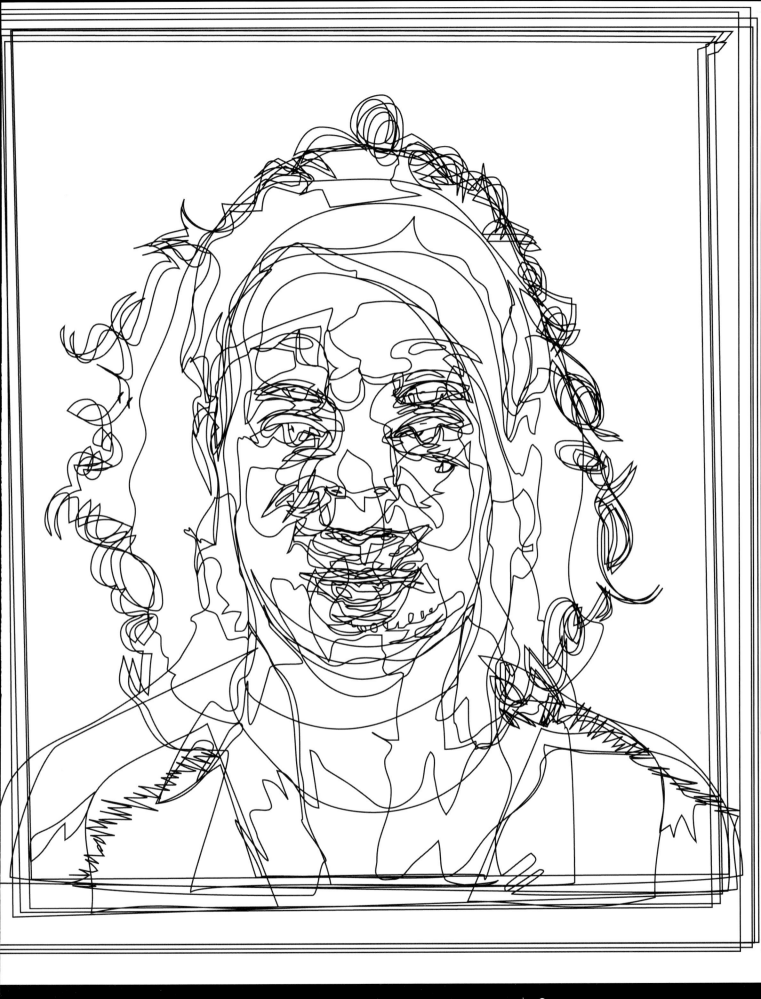

Pt 13 Design Firm: APT 13, Athens, Georgia (USA)
Creative Direction, Art Direction and Design: PHILLIP DWYER

Design Firm: **APT 13**, Athens, Georgia (USA)   Creative Direction, Art Direction and Design: P

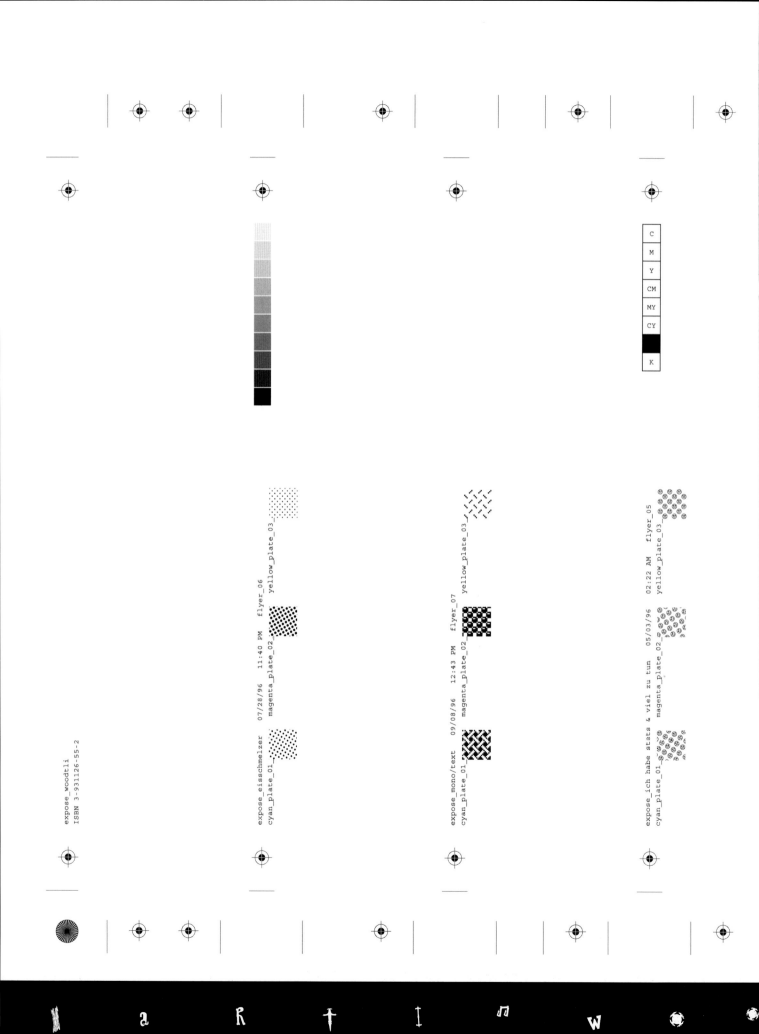

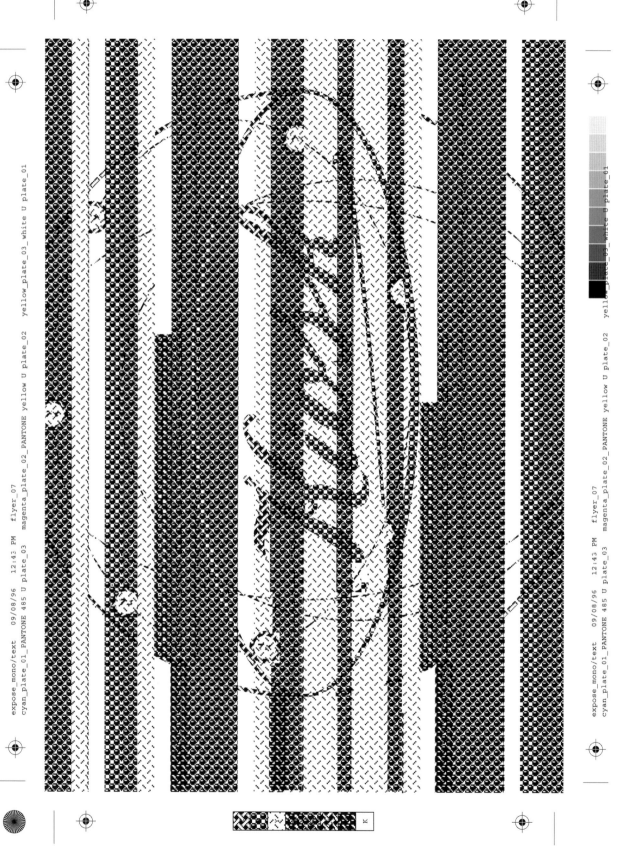

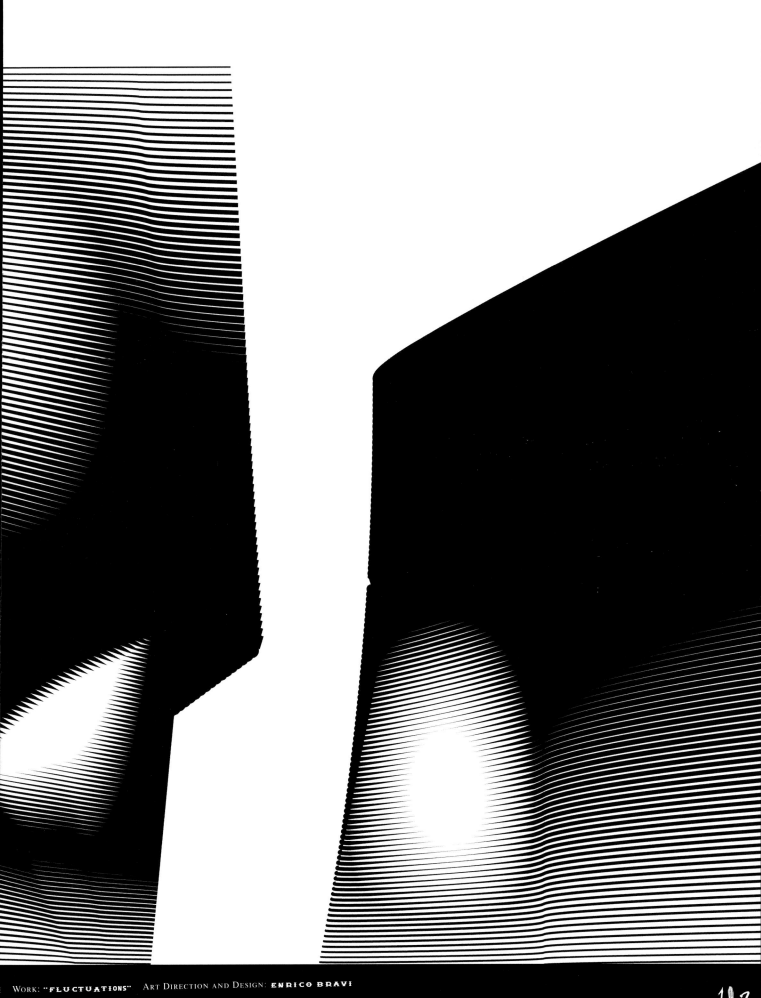

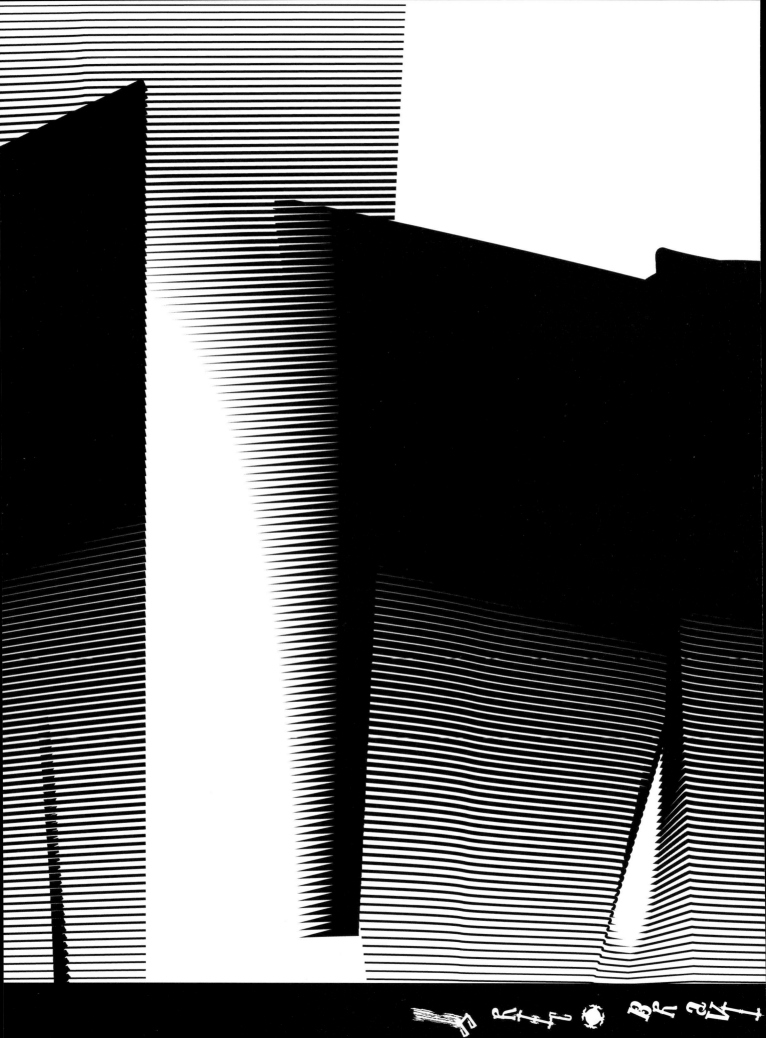

Design Firm: **ENRICO BRAVI**, VIENNA (AUSTRIA) Work: **"FLUCTUATIONS"** Art Direction and Design: **ENRICO BRAVI**

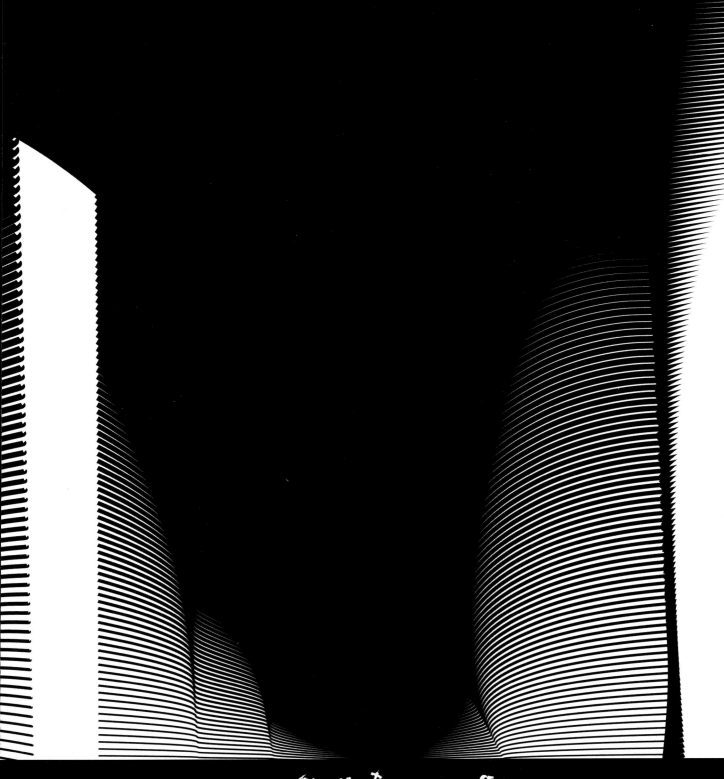

Design Firm: **TOMATO, LONDON (UK)** Art Direction and De
Layout: Lugli

AUTONOMIST
THE IMAGES ARE THEIR OWN TITLES

DESIGN: **SIMON** TAYLOR

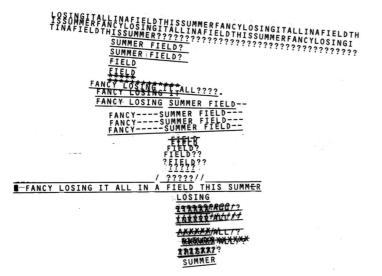

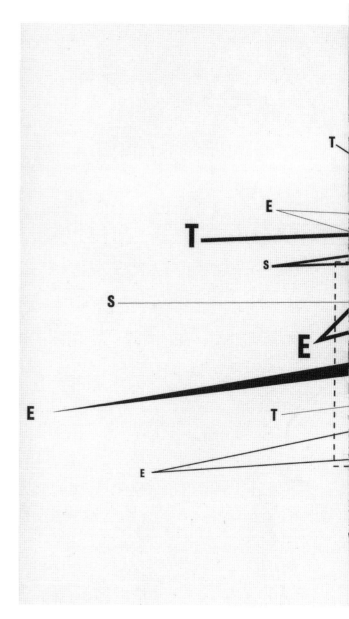

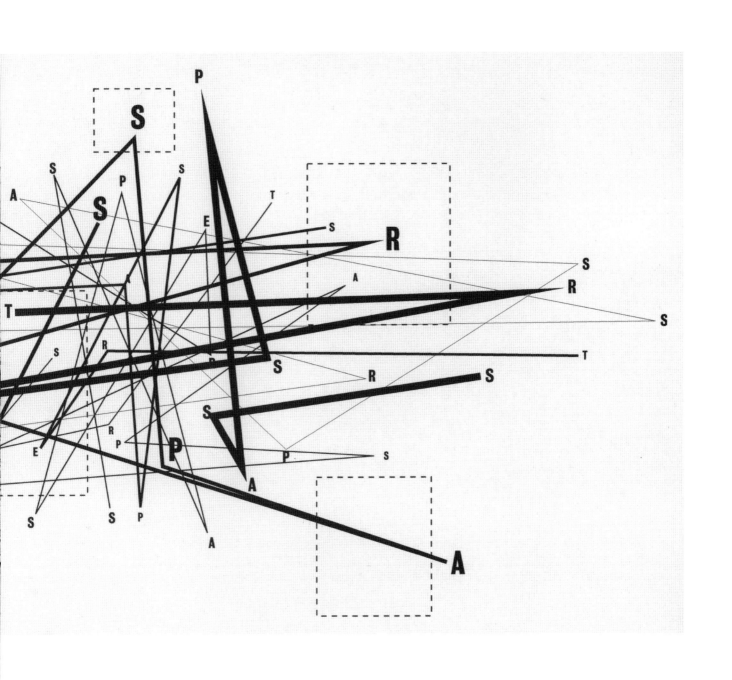

Design Firm: **TOMATO, LONDON (UK)** Work: **KINETIC** ART

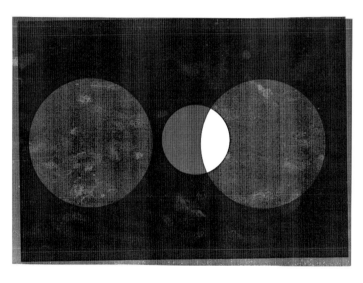

 Design Firm: **TOMATO, LONDON (UK)** Work:

(LEFT) X10X SCAN 01, PRAGUE CIRCLES, O+O O. (RIGHT) FALLEN ANGEL   ART DIRECTION AND DESIGN: SIMON TAYLOR

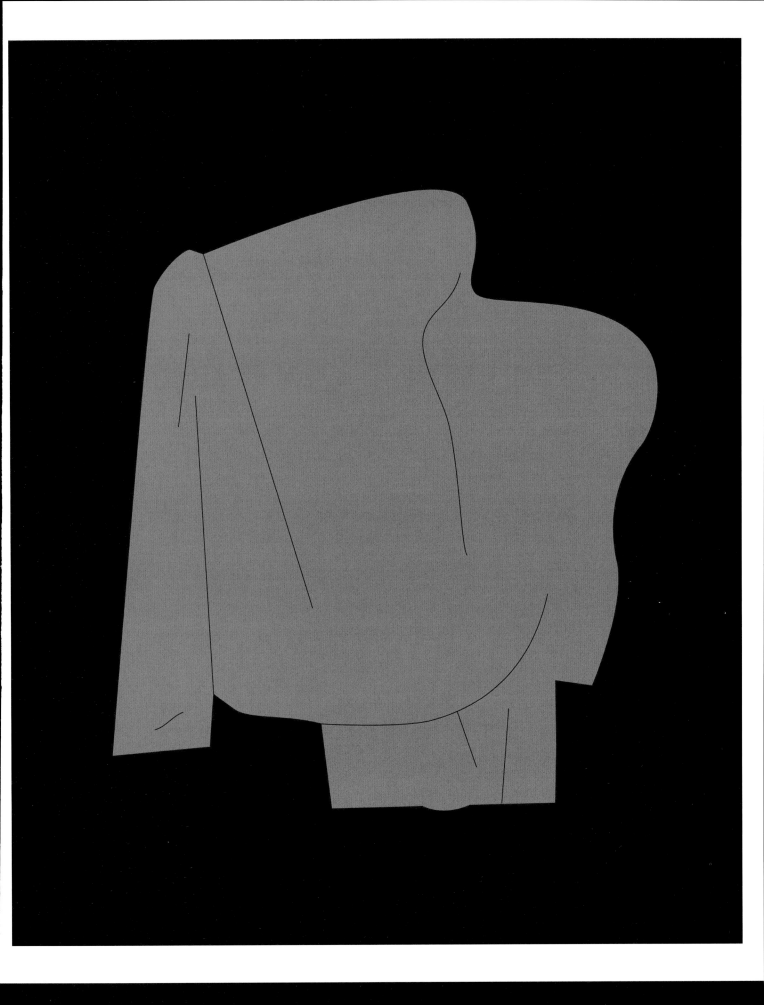

FORMAL / **EMBARRASSING 1—6**, sketches for **EXPERIMENTAL CLOTHES DESIGN**, 2002

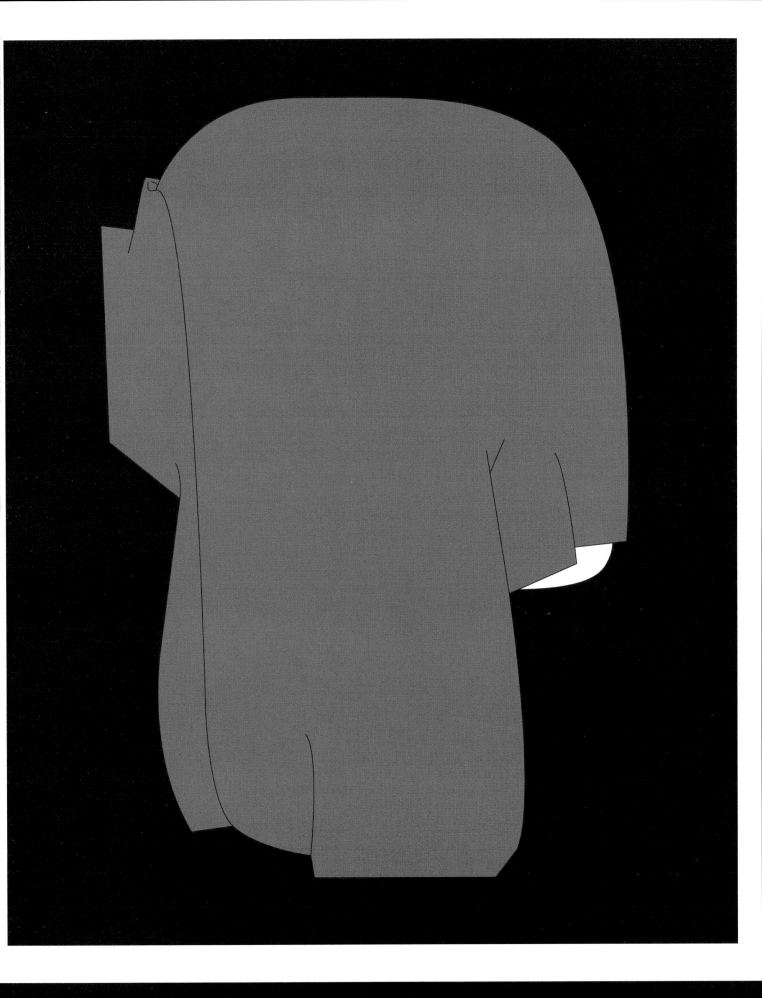

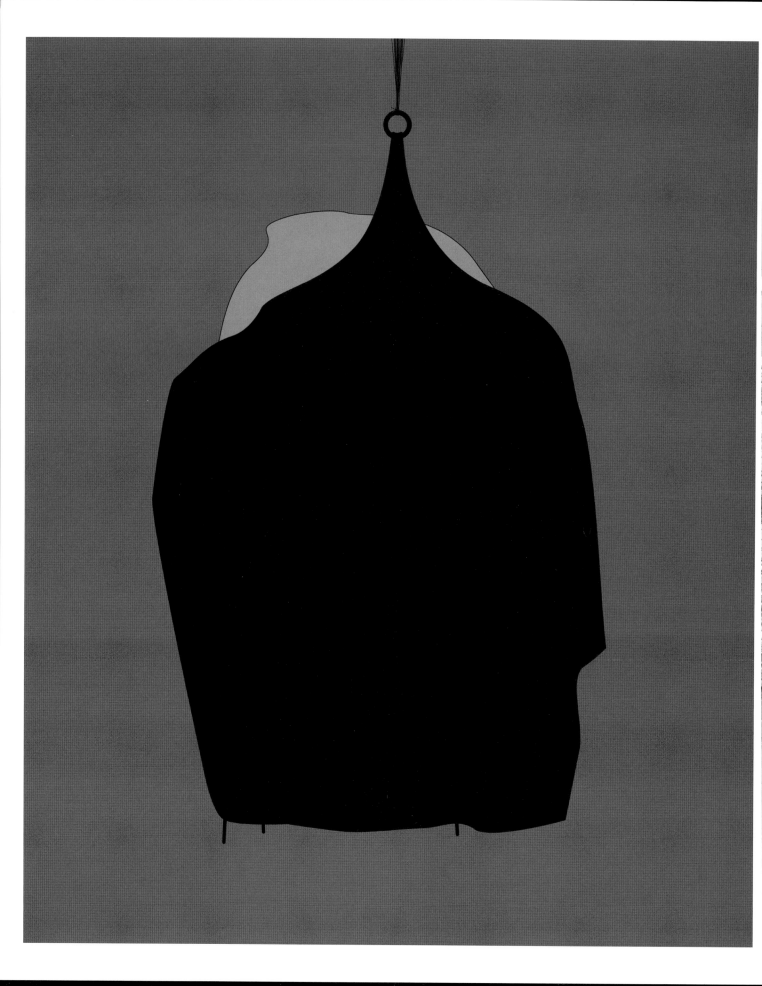

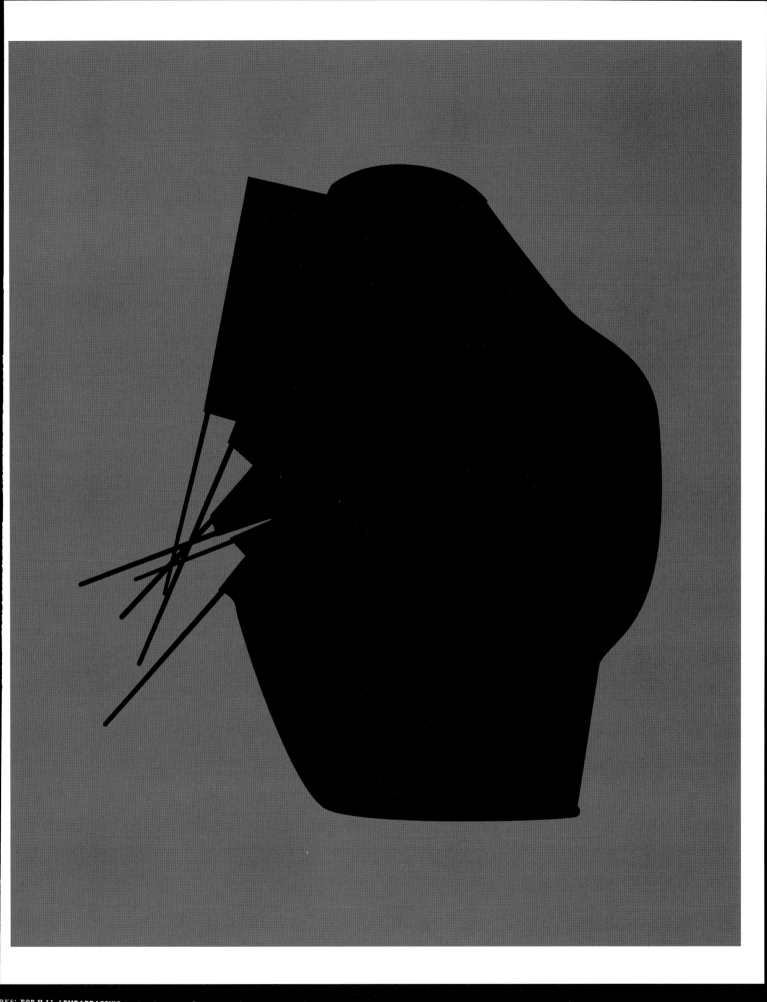

Design Firm: **Darren Scott** Typographics
Art Direction and Design: **Darren Scott**

DESIGN FIRM: **DARREN SCOTT TYPOGRAPHICS**, MANCHESTER (UK)
WORKS: THE BEAUTIFUL MACHINE (**SCOTT**: "This is a short movie which will be used to promote my Mechanic Text typeface. Working with **ROB BROWN** it helped me to explore a
CLIENT: **DARREN SCOTT TYPOGRAPHICS**   ART DIRECTION AND DESIGN: **DARREN SCOTT/ROB BROWN**   3D ANIMATION / MODELING AND ALLROUND TECHNICAL WIZARD

If that makes achieving Insight sound like a journey, it's meant to.

A journey to a place where consumers reveal, despite themselves, the complex mechanism of their *spirit*

Or where l o n g exhausted markets surrender new, exciting opportunities like a blink of **gold** in the pan.

DESIGN FIRM: **DARREN SCOTT TYPOGRAPHICS**, MANCHESTER (UK)
PHOTOGRAPHY: **JOHN SHARD**

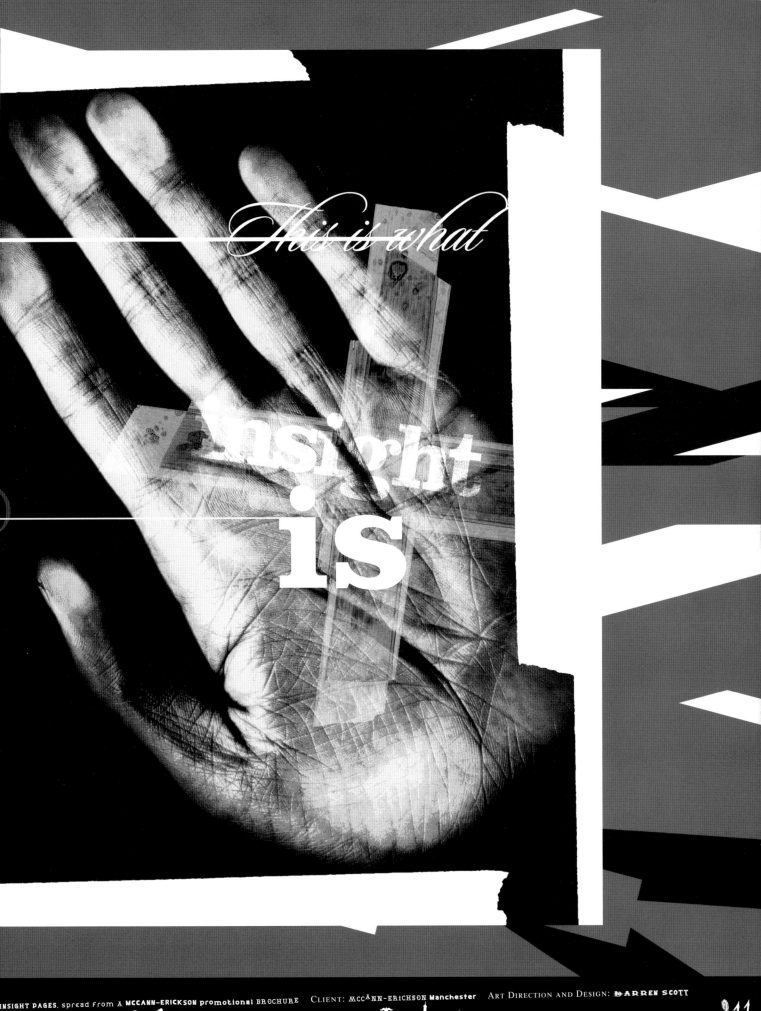

NEED A NEW FACE? YOU NEED AGGREGATE

A TYPEFACE BY DARREN SCOTT

NN-ERICKSON promotional BROCHURE, (RIGHT) AGGREGATE POSTER
N SCOTT TYPOGRAPHICS   ART DIRECTION AND DESIGN: DARREN SCOTT
PHOTOGRAPHY: JOHN SHARD, DARREN SCOTT   MODEL: Stuart Taylor

I'VE ALWAYS LOVED BLACK & WHITE, THE SIMP[

THAT'S NOT THE CASE OF BLACK & W
BEST WAY TO DISCOVER WHETHER HE TR[

THE MAIN INTENT OF THIS BO[
'CHROMATIC RESTRICTION' (IN COMPARISON TO FULL COLOUR) HAS A TRULY

IN THE WORLD OF FASHION BLACK EMBODIES
PRIESTS WEAR BLACK, WHILE THE GOTH BOYS

WHY SO? ISN'T BLACK THE [

BUT THIS DOESN'T MEAN TO BE A DEFENCE TO

T[
MAYBE THE BLACK COLOUR CAN TRULY
DO NOT KNOW ABOUT OURSELVES SCARES
OTHERWISE IT IS IN THE DARKNESS OF THEIR ROOMS THAT KIDS FR

BACKWORD

WHY TO DESIGN in BLACK AND WHITE.

AND **STRENGTH** OF A **BLACK SIGN** ON A WHITE BACKGROUND AND A **WHITE SIGN** ON BLACK. IT HAS ALWAYS FASCINATED ME, MUCH MORE THAN COLOUR.

DESIGN IN BLACK AND WHITE IS TURNING BACK TO THE **ORIGINS OF DESIGN**, TO ESSENTIAL ELEMENTS. THE COLOUR **EXCUSE** HAS OFTEN **HIDDEN POOR DESIGNERS**. IT HAS BEEN **THE** LARK-MIRROR FOR UNSKILLED AUDIENCE. **NO TRICK** THAT STANDS WITH BLACK & WHITE. FACING BLACK **AND** WHITE the designer is LEFT IN HIS NUDITY AND **THIS IS** THE HAS SOMETHING TO SAY. IT'S A COMPARISON WITH NUDITY. **THE ARTISTS** APPEARING IN THIS BOOK TURNED OUT QUITE COMFORTABLE WITH THEIR OWN.

IS TO RESTATE THE VALUE (IF IT HAD LOST SHINE IN ANY WAY) OF ONE COLOUR CREATIVITY BECAUSE WHAT IS CALLED MOUS EXPRESSIVE RICHNESS, FOUND IN THE VARIETY OF **SHADES OF GREY** AND IN THE **SHARP CONTRAST** OF BLACK AND WHITE.

BLACK.
DEEP BLACK.
A PLUNGE INTO BLACK.
A COLOUR **WHICH IS notably subject** TO PREJUDICE.

ASSAILABLE ELEGANCE, BUT IS MORE COMMONLY ASSOCIATED WITH death AND mourning IN MANY PEOPLE'S MINDS. **WIDOWS** AND LS STAND IN THEIR BLACK CLOTHES **OUT** IN THE STREETS. KILLERS IN MOVIES ALWAYS WEAR DARK COATS, AS USUAL **BLACK**, DARK HATS, BETTER **BLACK, AND**...GUESS, **BLACK GLOVES**.

IN THE COLLECTIVE IMAGINARY BLACK WON A **PARTICULAR NEGATIVE PLACE**.

R OF ELEGANCE PAR EXCELLENCE? ISN'T IT ONE OF THE **EASIER COLOURS TO MATCH**? FURTHER MORE IT MAKES you LOOK THINNER...

K TO THE BITTER END. AS A MATTER OF FACT IN THIS BOOK THERE'S MORE SPACE FOR WHITE THAN BLACK, AND IT MIGHT BE TITLED "WHY WHITE?" - TO UNDERLINE THE **IMPORTANCE OF THE BLANK SPACE** (I MEAN TO SAY THE "BREATH") IN A LAYOUT. BUT BLACK, AS FAR AS WHITE, INTERESTS ME A LOT.

RE CONSIDERED ANTITHETICAL BUT TO TELL THE TRUTH THEY'RE FLIP SIDES OF THE SAME COIN. THEY REPRESENT our INNER LIFE. MMARIZE HUMAN FEARS. DARKNESS, THAT METAPHORICALLY REPRESENT **THE UNKNOWN**, KEEPS SCARING US. AND WHAT WE MOST OF ALL, IF IT IS TRUE THAT EVERYONE OF US HAS A DARK SIDE. IF IT IS TRUE THAT THE EVIL COMES **FROM OUR INSIDE**. OVER THE WORLD **KEEP FEARING** GHOSTS AND MONSTERS, WHICH MIGHT APPEAR FROM UNDER THEIR BED AND **TAKE** THEM **AWAY**.

ANDREA LUGLI

CAROLINE ABELE
Caroline Abele lives in Stuttgart, Germany. After studies in Germanics and Art History in Heidelberg she is now a student of Visual Communications at the State Academy of Art and Design Stuttgart. In her work she shows a preference for ambiguous material-based objects to evoke individual associations instead of forcing obvious meaning. Her work includes several experimental typefaces, illustrations for the Dalliance booklet released by Emigre, a collaboration in the "AR book" - Report of Annual Reports and the codesign of the book "concept never ends". Samples were published/shown in PAGE and :output04. 140-145

URS ALTHAUS
Urs Althaus, 1973
Hausgrafik since 1999
86-91

APT 13
Phillip Dwyer (apt13) began working in a small two bedroom apartment in atlanta, ga, usa, during the summer of 1996. while in atlanta, apt13 worked primarily with the underground indie and punk music scene designing album covers and flyers for bands from around the world. in the summer of 1998, apt13 moved to brooklyn, ny to art direct a small clothing company. due to boredom and lack of creative freedom, apt13 left said clothing company after 6 months and has enjoyed a life of freelance bliss ever since, designing everything from album covers to snowboards to interactive media. recent clients have included Warner Bros Records, Priority Records, Platform Network, No Idea Records, Troubleman Unlimited, Buddy System Records, Simba Records, Polyvinyl Records, Goodfellow Records, Ferret Records, File13 Records, American Eagle Outfitters, Express Fashion, Tor Books, Burton Snowboards, Jager Di Paola Kemp, and more. apt13 has also been seen in the CodexSeries02 cd-rom (usa), IDN magazine (hong kong), Staf magazine (spain), +81 magazne (japan), IMGSRC100 (japan). 172-177

ROBERTO BAGATTI
Born in London, UK.
Studied at the Istituto D'Arte P. Toschi in Parma, Italy.
Works for MTV South.
80-85

ENRICO BRAVI
Enrico Bravi, born in Urbino (Italy) in 1975.
He studied Graphics at the Istituto Superiore per le Industrie Artistiche (ISIA) in Urbino from 1994 to 1998. In November 1998 he has been winner of the "First Daimler-Benz AG Graphic Illustration and Painting Competition". His work has been used in the world-wide print campaign for the Mercedes-Benz S-Class. From 1999 to 2002 he has collaborated as designer with Nofrontiere Design. One of his artworks, a vinyl album cover for the American band "The Walkabouts", has been selected to be part of the design permanent collection at the San Francisco Museum of Modern Art (SFMOMA). Designer and photographer, he lives and works in Vienna. 182-187

MARCUS BURLILE
Marcus Burlile was born in Columbus, Ohio in 1970 to a handsome, yet modest couple. From the introduction of letterforms as a young boy in elementary school, the art of graphics and lettering continues to grow as the greatest interest in his life. A majority of time is spent pursuing this desire. He studied art, design, and typography in La Jolla, California obtaining a bachelor's degree in design in 1992. His pursuit of self-exploration with type have currently yielded over one hundred digital fonts retailed worldwide by such type foundries as Garagefonts, [T-26], Fontworks UK, Fonthaus, Precision Type, AGFA, Atomic Type, Monotype, TypeUSA, Plazm Fonts, and 13 Types. Type experiments can also be seen expressed within his fine art paintings. As a design consultant and freelance art director for a vast portfolio of clients, his work has appeared within many national as well as international typography award books. 92-97

RUDY VANDERLANS [EMIGRE]
Rudy VanderLans has been publishing the design quarterly Emigre since 1984. Recently he published Supermarket, his first book of photographs exploring his love for Southern California. 14-19

SHEPARD FAIREY
Born in Charleston, South Carolina, February 15, 1970. 1989 First "Andre the Giant" sticker. 1991 started alternate graphics print studio. 1992 bfa degree Rhode Island School of Design. 1992-1996 ran alternate graphics and developed the Giant clothing / skateboard line, and propoganda movement. Posters for Giant and rock bands become the focus. 1995 filmmaker Helen Stickler makes documentary on Giant phenomenon. 1996 move to San Diego and meet Dave Kinsey and start Blk/Mrkt Design, focusing on graphics and marketing for the action sports and music industries. 1998-2000 "World Domination Tour" begins with an ambitious schedule of art shows and poster missions in almost every major U.S. city as well as London, Tokyo, Melbourne, and Hong Kong. Large billboard installations become standard procedure with well over 200 billboards liberated to date. 2001 Blm/Mrkt moves it's office to Los Angeles and opens its own gallery to showcase artists and designers. 2002 business as usual... rockin' in the semi-free world. 74-79

STEPHEN FARRELL

Stephen Farrell is principal and founder of Slipstudios, a venue established in 1992 to facilitate the research, writing, design and production of collaborative literature and visual essays, digital typography and ambient music. Farrell's projects—short stories, novellas, essays, performance readings and interactive digital works—have garnished numerous awards including two nominations for a Pushcart Prize, a National Design Award nomination in Communications from the Smithsonian Institute and the Tsujinaka Experimental Fiction Award of Kyoto. Farrell is finishing work on his first full-length imagetext novel, VAS, with writer Steve Tomasula. VAS explores biotechnology's strategies of representing the corporeal body and will be available from December 2002. Farrell is Assistant Professor of Design and Typography at The School of the Art Institute of Chicago. He graduated from The Ohio State University in Columbus, Ohio. 50-55

EDWARD FELLA

Edward Fella is a graphic designer whose work has had an important influence on contemporary typography in US and Europe. He practiced professionally as a commercial artist in Detroit for 30 years before receiving an MFA in design from the Cranbrook Academy of Art in 1987. He has since devoted his time to teaching and his own unique self-published work which has appeared in many design publications and anthologies. In 1997 he received the Chrysler Award and in 1999 an Honorary Doctorate from CCS in Detroit. His work is in the National Design Museum and MOMA in New York.
His type "Outwest" and dingbats "Fella Parts" are available from Emigre. A book of his photographs & lettering "Letters On America" was published in 2000. 20-25

ERIC FENG

Education: School of Visual Arts, New York. Major: computer & traditional Animation. Art Director at Ogilvy & Mather (94-96). Production Designer for Sprite Entertainment. Conceptual designer for Square USA (2000-2002), projects: Matrix 2 DVD, Astor Boy presentation. Final Fantasy: The sprit within (movie). Founder of Feric design studio (New York) 1999.
His work is featured in publications such as Pictoplasma (Die Gestalten Verlag), Etapes Graphic magazine, IDN (International Designer Network). 164-169

GESINE GROTRIAN-STEINWEG

1967 born in Braunschweig. Assistant in Fotostudios and Praktika in Advertising, Graphic and Print. Studied Visual Communication at the University of applied Science Düsseldorf, Diploma 1995. Assistant to Illustration Professor Wolf Erlbruch. Worked as Illustrator and Graphic Designer in Düsseldorf 1995 to 1999 and in1999 lectures in Typografie at the University in Essen, opening a studio in Berlin in 2000. September 2001 Founded the company Fons Hickmann m23 together with Simon Gallus and Fons M. Hickmann. Gesine served as guest professor Typografie at University in Essen, 2001. Lives and works together with Uma Malina, born 2000, and Fons in Berlin and Vienna. 170-171

BENJAMIN GÜDEL

Born 1968 - in Bern, Switzerland
1990-1994 - studies Graphic Design
1998 onwards: self-employed as illustrator in Zuerich, Switzerland. 158-163

DAVID ZACK CUSTER [HANDGUN]

Born: Billings, Montana 45°49'20"N 108°22'42"W. School: Associate of Science in Design, Northwest College, Powell, Wyoming 44°45'26"N 108°45'31"W. School: Bachelor of Arts in Design, Minneapolis College of Art and Design, Minneapolis, Minnesota 44°57'46"N 93°17'50"W. Intern: Studio d Design, Minneapolis, Minnesota 44°57'20"N 93°17'49"W. Work: Charles S. Anderson Design Co./CSA Images, Minneapolis, Minnesota 45°00'27"N 93°15'34"W. Freelance: HandGun, Minneapolis, Minnesota/Portland, Oregon 45°00'27"N 93°15'34"W/45°32'11"N 122°39'7"W. Work: Adidas International, Portland, Oregon 45°32'11"N 122°39'7"W. Freelance: Manual, Portland Oregon 45°32'11"N 122°39'7"W. 122-127

FRANK HEINE [U.O.R.G.]

Frank Heine was born in 1964. Before entering the State Academy of Fine Arts in Stuttgart, Germany, he had already completed several internships with silk screen and offset printers. During his studies Heine was employed at a graphic studio, where he worked intensively on corporate identities and graphic design/typography for museums and exhibitions. Since 1991 Heine is continually designing new typefaces that are distributed through several foundries. Among his designs are the well-known Remedy, Amplifier and Dalliance. In 1994 he founded his own company, U.O.R.G. in Stuttgart. Besides the design of new fonts and typo-graphic logos, the company focuses on corporate design, brochures, posters, museums and exhibitions. Heine's work has been published in novum, Emigre magazine, Page, IDEA magazine, Graphis Digital Fonts I, Emotional Digital, Typography 17 and 20, Creative Impulse 6. He is a member of BDG (the German association of graphic designers), the German "Forum Typography" and of the TDC New York. 128-133

FONS M. HICKMANN

Fons M. Hickmann was Born somewhere among the coal heaps of the Ruhr area. Afflicted by bouts of typographic fever, since falling into a bowl of alphabet soup as a child. 1972 beginning of school career spent on soccer pitches between Dortmund and Schalke. Travels in distant lands. 1987 start attempts at studying philosophy, Germanic philology, photography, art and design, leading to a diploma in graphic design. In 1991, crowned as "Guaredish the First" by the Düsseldorf Typographic Society and dubbed Typographic Knight for Life. Established design offices in Düsseldorf and Berlin in 1995, with virtual stations in Dortmund and Essen. Currently, "Fons Hickmann m23" in Berlin. 1997 appointments as a lecturer and professor at various universities, lecture tours, participation in juries, numerous publications. Received innumerable design awards and honours. Member of TDC, ADC, AGD and ABC. In 2001, appointment to the University of Applied Arts in Vienna in 2001, as professor in the areas of "Cognitive Dissonances", "All Media" and "Applied Soccer". 134-139

KIM HIORTHØY

Born in Trondheim, 1973. studied at The Academy Of Fine Art in Trondheim 1991-1996, School Of Visual Art, New York 1994-1995, Royal Academy Of Art, Copenhagen 1999-2001. Started out as a freelance illustrator and graphic designer ca. 1993 and has designed numerous record covers, posters, book jackets and illustrated several children's books since then. A monograph, Tree Weekend, was published by Die Gestalten Verlag in 2000.   198-203

GEOFF KAPLAN [GENERAL WORKING GROUP]

Geoff Kaplan is the principle of General Working Group, located in San Francisco. General Working Group's practice is focused on academic and cultural institutional work including; Cranbrook Academy of Art, CalArts, MOCA, The Walker Art Center, UCLA, Woodbury University, and the AIA. Several projects by Kaplan are in SFMOMA's permanent design collection. He currently teaches in the Graduate Design program at CCAC. Kaplan's work will be featured in "Le mois du graphisme d'Echirolles" California design in France. Kaplan received his MFA from Cranbrook Academy of Art.   116-121

DEAN KARR

When speaking of Director/Photographer Dean Karr, the one thing that people seem to agree on is that he is a true original. His signature style, often copied but never duplicated, has gained him international recognition as one of a small group of young media artists whose work interprets and defines our time. Dean Karr's prolific work as a music video/commercial director, and his cutting edge photographic images, have brought him to the forefront of his craft. His directorial work, with artists such as Marilyn Manson, the Dave Matthews Band, the Deftones, Ozzy Osbourne, Dr. Dre, B Real, Duran Duran and John Forte with Wyclef Jean, reveals a highly-tuned sense of style, fashion, art, and storytelling. His music videos are constantly found at the top of MTV playlists, and have been nominated for major MTV, Billboard, and MVPA Video Awards in each of the last three years, ("Don't Drink the Water" by the Dave Matthews Band was nominated for the 1998 "Best Rock Video" and "Best Cinematography" Awards).   104-115

ANDREA LUGLI

1990-1993 studied philosophy at Bologna University.
Freelance designer since 1997.
In 2001 edited the book "Creative Impulse 6", a design firms selection.
In 2002 started Crucix-Shop project.
44-49, 62-69, 104-115, 188-197, 204-213

MAROK [LODOWN]

Born in 1972 and raised in Berlin. Occupation: visual wizardary. Studied graphic design from 1991-1994, and in 1994 started a street orientated clothing label called 'Umd'. All along Marok's core focus was to seek work as a graphic designer and in 1994 and 1995 worked in the USA in without a greencard. In 1995 he founded Lodown magazine, inspired by his experience with David Carson at Raygun Magazine in California. 1995-2001 Marok produced work for companies which alowed unorthodox styles. Other projects include the 1997 production of the first video for Lodown called Super108, all filmed in super8, a five city exhibition tour in 1998 with Futura2000, called 'Reproduced98'. 1998 also saw the release of several video projects for the music industry. 1999 brought the co-founding the Lodown online project and the publication of the first Lodown-all graphics-book, called 'Lodown Engineering'. In 2001 the follow-up project called 'Schizophrenic-Lodown Engineering part 2' was published. 2001 also saw the release of graphic exhibitions all over the planet including Sidney, Birmingham and Cologne. In 2002 the Lodown sneaker project with Etnies was released along with another graphic publication called M Transforming Language.   70-77

PLANET PIXEL
[ANJA WÜLFING, OLIVER FUNKE]

Anja Wülfing, born 13th Nov. 1969, Cologne, Germany. Education: 1985-1987 -> A Levels in Design. 1987-1989 -> Apprenticeship at Advertising Agency (K&K Cologne). 1989-1992 -> Bachelor of Fine Arts at Art Center College of Design (Europe/Switzerland). Professional Experience: 1992-1995 -> Freelancer/Graphic Designer/Art Director at Werbeagentur Pütz (Cologne), Negelken&Negelken (Cologne), Gratzfeld Werbeagentur (Cologne). 1995 -> Founded Planet Pixel.

Oliver Funke, born: 9th. April 1968, Worms, Germany. Education: 1989-1992 -> Bachelor of Fine Arts at Art Center College of Design (Europe/Switzerland). Professional Experience: 1992-1993 -> Graphic Designer/Art Director at K+K Werbeagentur (Cologne), Gratzfeld Werbeagentur (Cologne). 1995 -> Founded Planet Pixel.   152-157

PLAZM

Plazm Media publishes an eclectic design magazine with worldwide distribution and operates an innovative type foundry. Plazm is also a design firm that builds complete brands, advertising and retail marketing plans using custom typography.
Clients include Lucasfilm, MTV and Nike. Plazm was founded in 1991 by artists as a creative resource, and celebrates its twelfth anniversary this year.   98-103

RAFFAELE PRIMITIVO

Raffaele Primitivo was born in 1971 in Ancona, Italy, where he attended the Centro Sperimentale Design, graduating as Fashion Creative and Visual Designer. In 1993 he started a career as freelance designer, working on a number of projects, amongst them the first catalogue for the newly launched brand Nose. In 1995, he joined the agency responsible for the image of Nose. When the agency was merged with Fornari to become Fornari Advertising Office in 1996, he became responsible for the visual design of the four Fornari brands: Fornarina, Nose, Brain and Barleycorn. Over the years Raffaele expanded his duties, becoming graphic designer and creative director for the newly launched free magazine Sni:z and an active member of the creative team for the design of Nose Clothing. Since 1999 Raffaele has art directed all the covers and advertising materials for Italian band Marlene Kuntz. He has always had a keen interest in music and dj'ing. Currently he is involved in the Hydra Project, a club-oriented dj act, both as a dj and promoter through his graphic design.   146-151

DIRK RUDOLPH

1964 birth - 1974 first camera - 1978 second camera and own darkroom - 1980 first band: bass and vocals in garage band „tag der milch" - design of first cassette sleeve for own band (record breaking sales of 14 copies) - design and publishing of own fanzine - 1982 second band „die sauberen drei" (the clean three) - 1983 third band fenton weills (named after non-famous german guitar builder) - first record release and single cover designs - 1984 schools out - 1985 opening an independent record shop - start and end of studying history and politics - 1986 founding a record label with a few friends, a few sleeve and poster designs working as a silkscreen printer to make some money - 1987 first design for polydor records (phillip boa and the voodooclub - copperfield - 1989 first apple computer - 1989 running an own business as a graphic designer and photographer - 1999 publishing of first book SPARK (die gestalten verlag) - 2001 first exhibition (oslo). 26-31

STEFAN SAGMEISTER

Stefan Sagmeister, a native of Austria, received his MFA in graphic design from the University of Applied Arts in Vienna and, as a Fulbright Scholar, a master's degree from Pratt Institute in New York.
He formed the New York based Sagmeister Inc. in 1993 and has since designed graphics and packaging for the Rolling Stones, David Byrne, Lou Reed, Aerosmith and Pat Metheny. His work has been nominated four times for the Grammies and has won most international design awards. In 2001 monograph about his work titled "Sagmeister, Made you Look" was published by Booth-Clibborn editions. 62-69

DARREN SCOTT

After graduating from Salford University in Manchester with a B.A. in Design Practice in 1996, Scott joined McCann-Erickson as a Designer and Typographic Consultant. Working for such a large agency gives him the opportunity to get involved in all aspects of the industry and the benefits of dealing with international blue chip clients. As a student Darren experimented with typeface design, and he was asked to develop a typeface for digital type magazine FUSE 15 [cities], which led to Berlin[er] his first digital font. The love affair with visible language developed from there. Since then Scott has developed several typefaces which are distributed by [T-26] in Chicago. and Atomic Type in London. As well as designing custom corporate typefaces. 204-213

JENNIFER STERLING

Jennifer Sterling, an AGI member, is principal of Sterling Design, an award-winning design studio based in San Francisco, specializing in print, interactive and product design. Jennifer serves on the SFMOMAs Architecture and Design Accessions Board, and in 2000 was invited to be a member of The National Registry of Who is Who in America. The SFMOMA recently hosted a three month solo exhibit of her work. Her work has also been exhibited in New York at the Smithsonian's Cooper-Hewitt National Triennial and is part of the permanent collections of the Library of Congress, The Smithsonian Cooper-Hewitt National Design Museum, Museum Fur Kunst Und Gewerbe Hamburg, The San Francisco Museum of Modern Art and Bibliotheque Nationale de France. Her work regularly appears in Communication Arts, ID, Type Directors Club, Graphis, the AIGA and other award publications. In 2000 and 2001 Jennifer won the Margaret Larsen award for best design in the San Francisco Advertising Show. Additionally she won Best of Show in 2000 and 2001 and The Walter Landor award for Design. Clients include branding for a coalition under the direction of Hillary Clinton and Madelaine Albright, Vertu, Nokia, and Yahoo along with the launch of her own product line. 56-61

GAIL SWANLUND

Gail Swanlund's LA studio produces award-winning projects for print and the Web. Her work has been exhibited at The San Francisco Museum of Modern Art, and most recently in "New Acquisitions: Experimental Design." She has been recognized by the American Center for Design, American Institute of Graphic Arts, and The Type Directors Club; her work is featured in Emigre, Eye, Print, IdN, and Zoo, and published in various design anthologies, including "Graphic Radicals, Radical Graphics," "The Graphic Edge," and "Typographics 4." She cut her teeth writing for the experimental and influential typography journal Emigre. Swanlund received her MFA from CalArts and teaches at UCLA and CalArts. 32-37

TOMATO

Tomato was formed in 1991 by Steve Baker, Dirk Van Dooren, Karl Hyde, Rick Smith, Simon Taylor, John Warwicker and Graham Wood. Gregory Rood joined in 1992 and left in 1996. Jason Kedgley joined in 1994. Dylan Kendle joined in 1995 and left in 1996. Michael Horsham joined in 1996.
In its eleven years of existence Tomato has built an international reputation for creative excellence in a variety of media including film, television advertising, identity design and communication strategies. The nine-member, london-based group also exhibits its non-commercial work regularly in cities all around the world - and has created and curated many different installation / exhibitions in places as far apart as Brno and Tokyo. 188-197

WHY NOT ASSOCIATES

Why Not Associates are a multi-disciplinary design studio creating highly innovative and varied work.
Established over twelve years ago, they believe that their vision and ideas can be applied to a wide range of media. Their optimistic and experimental attitude has led to projects ranging from designs for postage stamps to large scale exhibitions and installations, via publishing, corporate identity, public art and moving image.
Clients include Nike, The Royal Mail, Malcolm Mclaren, The Pompidou Centre, The Royal Academy Of Arts and Lincoln Cars. 38-43

MARTIN WOODTLI

1971 born in Berne, living and working in Zurich; 1990 - 95 School of Design Berne, graphic design; 1996 - 98 Zurich Academy of Art and Design, Visual communication; 1998 - 99 stay in N.Y worked by Stefan Sagmeister; 1999 Open his Studio in Zurich - 1999 Swiss Federal Design Prize; 2000 I.D. Magazine «The I.D. Forty» NY, USA; 2000 Getting Member by AGI (Alliance Graphique International); 2001 IDEA 285, Tokyo, Japan; 2001 kAk Magazine, Moskau, U.S.S.R.; 2001 Book „woodtli" „Die Gestalten Verlag", Berlin, Germany; 2002 Prize for "The Most Beautiful Swiss Books". 178-181

CAROLINE ABELE
Lehenstraße 27
70180 Stuttgart
Germany
Phone +49.711.2567156
Email c.abeleAT instanthome.de

URS ALTHAUS
Schöneggstrasse 5
CH-8004 Zürich, Swiss
Phone: +41 79 204 16 50
Fax: +41 1 241 06 73
ursAThausgrafik.ch
www.hausgrafik.ch

APT13
www.apt13.com

ROBERTO BAGATTI
rbagattiATyahoo.it

ENRICO BRAVI
Josefstaedter Strasse 74/4b
1080 Vienna – Austria
Tel. +43 1 9902860
e-mail: urbinautaATmac.com

MARCUS BURLILE
9040 Falcon Glen Court
Bristow, Virginia 20136 – U.S.A.
phone: 1-571-330-5290
email: KreativSpiritATyahoo.com

RUDY VANDERLANS [EMIGRE]
Emigre
4475 D Street
Sacramento, CA 95819 – USA
www.emigre.com

SHEPARD FAIREY
WWW.OBEYGIANT.COM and WWW.BLKMRKT.COM
AGENT/MANAGER CONTACT: AMANDA AYALA FAIREY
3780 WILSHIRE BLVD. STE.210, LOS ANGELES, CA 90010 USA
213-383-9299 X.11 or amandaATobeygiant.com

STEPHEN FARRELL
Slipstudios
4421 North Francisco Avenue
Chicago, Illinois 60625 USA
ph. 773.279.0979
e. slipstudiosATcompuserve.com

ED FELLA
CalArts, California Institute of the Arts, USA

ERIC FENG
57 Jay st roomNo. 6a Brooklyn, New York 11201 U.S.A.
Phone: 1 (808) 535-9041
www.feric.com

GESINE GROTRIAN-STEINWEG
Hetzgasse 45.11 A 1030 Wien
0043.1.7143814 – Fax 7143815
grotrianATkairos.to

BENJAMIN GÜDEL
benjaminATguedel.biz
www.guedel.biz

HANDGUN
David Zack Custer
1210 NE Hancock Street Apt. F, Portland, OR 97212 USA
503-358-3486
zackAThand-gun.org
www.hand-gun.org

FRANK HEINE
U.O.R.G.
Reinsburgstrasse 96 A 70197 Stuttgart Germany
Phone +49.711.6567.9993 – Fax +49.711.6567.9995
Email frankATuorg.com
www.uorg.com

FONS M. HICKMANN
Mariannenplatz 23, Gartenhaus D 10997 Berlin Germany
T 004930.69518501
fonsATfonshickmann.de

Type

Lilyin Castiron
Lilyin Regular

LILYIN SAGUARO
LILYIN TARNISH

Lilyin Tupelo

Lilyin Wanted

"Lilyin Family" is a font designed by Marcus Burlile, available from Plazm Fonts (www.plazm.com).

DEAD MULE CANION
DEAD MULE GRANDE
DEAD MULE WEST

"Dead Mule Family" is a font designed by Marcus Burlile, available from T-26 (www.t26.com).

THE SOUTH SIDONIE

"The South Sidonie" is a type designed by Andrea Lugli in 1997, based upon the "Quentin" woodtype.

The Black&Why#1 Typeface

"The Black&Why#1 Typeface" is a custom made type designed by Andrea Lugli in 2002, based upon the "Antique Tuscan No.8" woodtype and the "Clarendon Bold" typeface.